Excel

HSC

ESSAY WRITING MADE EASY

SECOND EDITION

STEPHEN McLAREN

MA Syd, Dip Ed, BA (Comms)

PASCAL
PRESS

Thanks to Sylvia Huntington for her helpful suggestions and patient reading.

Copyright © 1995 S. McLaren
Reprinted 1996, 1997, 1998, 2000
Second edition 2001
Reprinted 2002

ISBN 1 74020 280 5

Pascal Press
PO Box 250
Glebe NSW 2037
(02) 8585 4044
http://www.pascalpress.com.au
Publisher: Vivienne Petris Joannou
Editor: Ken Tate
Typeset by *Diℓ/gn*.
Cover by *Diℓ/gn*.
Cartoons by Grant McAloon
Printed in Singapore by Green Giant Press

Contents

Chapter by
chapter contents

Reading and language (read read read, write write write)

    Critics and commentaries

Some language terms

Figures of speech

Preface to

second edition

It is a great pleasure to introduce the second edition of this book, which has been comprehensively revised for the new HSC syllabus. As with the first edition, the focus stays on the HSC English syllabus, which remains a core compulsory subject. Writing skills are essential to each level of our academic development and I believe that this book is of equal value to English Extension students as it is to those who are studying other courses in English.

Given the continuing demand for the first edition since 1995, clearly there was a real need for help with the skills of formal writing. Under the new HSC this need remains. While the standards-referenced approach to assessment does not emphasise essay-writing skills as such, writing well pays off in every subject that involves formal writing or extended responses. That is because an essay can only be as good as the quality of thought that informs it, and writing helps you to develop your understanding of the subject. Good, clear writing is the sign of a good understanding of the topic.

Under the new HSC syllabus, students doing Standard English need to perform very well to achieve the top levels of assessment banding, whereas Advanced and Extension English students will find significant expectations of their composing skills. According to a key policy document:

Students undertaking standard courses will have the opportunity to perform well up the scale, but they will be less likely to do so than those successfully undertaking more advanced work. Students undertaking more demanding studies, therefore, will be rewarded for their hard work and performance. The rewards, however, will not be automatic: they will depend on success in meeting the standards.

(*Securing Their Future*, NSW Government, 1997, p.24.)

Clearly the new HSC has been devised to reward achievement, and good writing is intrinsic to that endeavour in most subjects.

The revision has been very substantial. Two of the three sample essays are new, to reflect the new syllabus. They have been composed for the Area of Study common to Standard and Advanced English, so will be of interest to most students. Sample questions, exercises and other references have all been updated to reflect the new syllabuses. I have retained the light tone of the original edition, and the use of contractions ('it's' rather than 'it is', 'don't' rather than 'do not') but students will appreciate that academic writing follows different rules and that many teachers frown on the use of contractions.

Development of the new HSC involved much effort to identify key competencies and outcomes which are central to workplace-readiness. I remain convinced that effective writing is one of the most important of these, and that taking time to develop one's writing skills remains one of the best 'investments' for the future that any student can make.

Stephen McLaren

To the reader

This book offers:

- A practical, commonsense introduction to essay writing for beginners, starting from the ground up
- An understanding of what writing essays is all about: not just what to do, but why!
- Helpful exercises to build up your skills
- Sample essays, dissected, with explanations
- Many examples!
- An opportunity to develop essay-writing skills at the same time as you study
- A detailed, step-by-step beginner's essay-writing method
- Special help with writing essays for English.

This book is designed for beginners, for people whose skills have become rusty, and anyone struggling with essay writing. The methods described here have been used successfully not only with battling students, but also with middling and even top students wanting to realise more of their potential.

I have been teaching English and writing skills for many years now and this book is based on the lessons I have learnt from students themselves: about what problems they encounter and what they need to know. No magic solutions or shortcuts are offered here, but you will find plenty of help in these pages. In particular I seek to dispel some common myths:

- You have to be a 'born' writer.
- You can't *learn* to write.
- I'm a bad writer: I can't spell.

This book allows you to begin from your own level of skill, and to build up slowly.

HSC students

For many HSC students, essay writing is both the greatest stumbling block, and a key to success — not just now, but later in life too. This book demonstrates that you should begin your year's study effort as early as possible, and that you can combine essay writing practice with study in different subjects, to 'kill two birds with one stone'. Particular attention is given to essays for HSC English, because it is a compulsory subject.

What's in this book?

- Section One gives some essential background about study, the writing process, and essays in particular.
- Section Two shows how to slowly build up your essay-writing skills, giving you practice with a number of 'microskills' first, before bringing all those skills together in an organised approach.
- Section Three describes ways of treating the specific requirements of essay writing for English.
- Section Four looks at exam essays and gives some hints about the special requirements of other subjects.

How to use this book

- Write a little each day.
- Get a reader/mentor.
- Become your own mentor (instead of tormentor).
- Do your writing exercises on topics you are studying.

Development of essay-writing skills takes time and regular practice. It is better to write a little each day (maybe for fifteen minutes) than to write for several hours once a week. Fix a set time for writing each day and stick to this, no matter what tempting diversions offer themselves. Take the phone off the hook, lock yourself in a room, put a 'Do Not Disturb' sign on the door if you have to!

Writing is often a lonely business and can be especially hard for an underconfident person. One trap for beginners is to become too harsh a critic of your own writing, throwing out promising drafts and discarding good ideas, instead of refining and polishing those rough beginnings.

Another common trap is trying to rewrite an essay according to what you imagine the teacher wanted, what a friend has done, or based on some other piece you've just read. (Maybe someone else's essay that an email chat friend has sent you.)

Not everyone can afford a tutor, although a good tutor can be invaluable. It will certainly be a great help to find a patient, supportive reader for your essay drafts: a parent, willing teacher or friend. You'll be surprised how much a perceptive reader can help you work through those ideas still trapped in a web of vague thoughts and hard-to-find words.

Or they can show you that what seems perfectly clear to you is not clear at all to the reader. Over time you will learn to criticise your own writings positively, and edit them more objectively, to become your own 'mentor', not tormentor.

Essays aren't just about words and writing, they're about your knowledge and thoughts. Writing also develops your understanding of topics; indeed, it is a skill that develops your mind! You don't have to wait to get a class essay before using this book — start doing the 'microskill' exercises in Chapter 4 now, then practise writing essays on topics you are currently studying, so that your understanding of study areas will grow as your skills do.

You can use this book for future reference too: if you are getting feedback from your teachers that your conclusions are weak, or that you need to write topic sentences, you can refer back to these specific points and find help.

sectionone:

Essential background

Introduction

Staffroom gossip: common teacher complaints about students

Let's hear some choice gossip from the staffroom. About you!

Crime 1:

You don't answer the question (you use a prefabricated, one-size-fits-all essay, and pretend that this answers the question, or you just waffle on about anything vaguely related to the topic).

Crime 2:

You have a good understanding of the subject, but still 'can't write an essay' (structure's all over the place).

Crime 3:

You write too little (what you write is good, but how can I give you top marks if you don't say half as much as another student?).

Crime 4:

You keep repeating yourself instead of developing your ideas further (you've got nothing more to say, you're wasting paper and ink ... and my time!).

Crime 5:

You have poor expression and use language badly (I can't even understand this!).

Crime 6:
You 'all write the same answer' (a bit of originality or imagination wouldn't go astray, in English at least).

Crime 7:
You can't spell.

You have probably committed some or all of these 'crimes'. The following chapters will help give you some insights into why these complaints are problems, and what to do about them. Please note that I have put spelling at the end of the heap ... It is significant, but it's not the most important thing by any means. Some students think that if they can't spell they can't write. Don't believe it; spelling is largely memory work, and definitely not a measure of your intelligence! But certainly, accurate spelling makes a good impression.

Experience has taught me that beginner essay writers most often need help in four main areas:

- How to study
- The process of writing
- Requirements of an essay
- Using language.

How to study

The quality of your essays depends on the quality of your study effort: you can't write in a vacuum. Although this is not a 'How to Study' book, we look at broad study issues in Chapter 1, while Chapter 5 focuses on studying for essays. The Thesis Essay Study Technique for English is an advanced study method based on essays, and can also be adapted to other subjects (see Chapter 7).

The process of writing

Writing is a gradual process: we develop that polished draft over time, building those patchy starts into a structured argument. A rough first draft is not a failure but a beginning. The writing process is discussed in Chapter 2.

Requirements of an essay

Essays make many demands, and a general description of these begins in Chapter 3.

Using language

Language use is extremely important to writing. It improves with practice; it improves draft by draft. Language is a subject vast enough to fill whole books. The focus here is restricted to a general awareness of language 'issues' such as clarity, word choice, and so on, rather than details of grammar and punctuation. Some of the more basic problems encountered by students are treated in this book, but if you want to study language in detail, you should consult some of the many good reference books available on grammar, punctuation, and spelling.

It is easy to get carried away with the importance of grammatical, fluent English, but this book emphasises meaning first: it's possible to write a grammatically perfect sentence that doesn't mean anything, and you can't find exactly the right words to express your thoughts until you know what you are really trying to say! The famous theorist Noam Chomsky produced this sentence for us to contemplate: 'Colourless green dreams sleep furiously'. Grammatically speaking, the sentence is perfect, but not only does it not seem to mean anything, it even contradicts itself — how can green dreams be colourless?

Essay writing for English...

This book devotes an entire section to English essays in particular. This is for several reasons:

- Many students find English the hardest subject, complaining that they don't understand what's expected of them.
- English is all about language. Essay writing helps develop your awareness of writing at the same time as you explore and develop ideas.
- A good essay in English uses all the fundamental skills that you could require in any subject, and once students get the hang of it, they usually notice an immediate improvement in essays for other subjects.
- The 'Thesis Essay' approach discussed in Section Three is a unique approach to English study which develops essay-writing skills, increases

your understanding of English texts and topics, and helps prepare you for the exams.

...And beyond

As they say in the Demtel ads: 'But there's more!' — the skills of writing you start to develop now will stand you in good stead when you go on to study at university or TAFE, and when you have to write letters and reports in your job. ('Communication skills' such as writing are much in demand with employers these days, a fact recognised in the new HSC syllabus.)

More important for the moment, increased proficiency in writing will help you enjoy your study better as your skills and your confidence increase.

Chapter 1

Essays and study

Essay writing can be compared to mountain climbing:

- It's an act of exploration.
- It takes preparation.
- Planning is important.
- It takes practice and discipline.
- You need to be 'fit'.
- You need agility.
- Particular skills are needed.

Like mountain climbing, essay writing has its ups and downs. Luckily, it's perfectly safe, so when you do suffer a mishap, you can just try again. An organised climb is planned carefully, enjoys steady progress and works past all the obstacles and difficulties one by one. And don't be like those thrill seekers who try to race up the slopes in one day, the day before the deadline, and can't work out why they run out of puff, strain something, overlook something vitally important, get holed up in a dead end without time to find a better path, or simply seize up with stress.

The climb is hard work — I'm sorry, like a mountain, there's no way around it — but an organised approach will make it bearable and more rewarding. Without this, your efforts will always be a bit of a scramble (in two senses of the word!) and you'll find it hard to get a secure foothold. With the necessary skills you can climb a very long way indeed, and the views from the top are just great! Honestly.

Exploration

Essay writing can and should be a learning process, a discovery of new territory. By writing about a subject, you will extend the frontiers of your understanding. You might find to your surprise that you've ended up writing a different essay to what you intended. Your ideas may have changed a lot, or even reversed completely in some cases, as you consider the evidence more carefully.

Preparation

You can't climb a mountain on an empty stomach; likewise, your mind requires good quality 'brain food': organised notes about your essay topics. Without sufficient knowledge, you can only write an empty essay.

Before planning your assault on 'Mount Everest', you need to research the job: just how tall, how treacherous, how cold is it up there? What gear will you need, what skills, how many provisions, how many team members? Be prepared!

Planning

It is preferable to plan any essay in advance, and this is essential in the exam room. However, it is possible to do some preliminary 'exploring' before coming up with a plan.

Equipment

You need a good, quiet study environment: a comfortable chair and desk, with good lighting. Get a good dictionary, a thesaurus, lots of manila folders or other folders for all your notes. Of course, computers are superb writing machines, since they make it easy to write and rewrite. An Internet connection also opens up the rich resources of the World Wide Web. (However, be wary about the reliability of Internet sites, and also be careful not to plagiarise — often a temptation. 'Plagiarise' means to copy someone else's work without acknowledging the true author. Even work which you download from the Internet should be referenced in terms of the author, site name and URL.)

Practice and discipline

Consider yourself a kind of study 'athlete': set your goals, train hard to achieve them, and check regularly that you are making satisfactory progress. It is much better to study efficiently, with concentration, for short bursts of time, than to spend many hours staring out the window. I know, I've tried both ways myself!

Professional writers speak of developing 'writing muscles' in the brain by regular practice. Certainly, the more frequently you write, the stronger will be your skills. Use your time carefully: by studying efficiently, you can earn time enough for fun, rest and recreation. Start early, concentrate hard for short bursts of time, take frequent breaks, and reward yourself for achieving goals.

Fitness

Various factors combine to make you 'fit'. The main thing is to keep up the writing effort consistently. It's amazing how quickly our skills start to get 'rusty' when we don't use them for a while. Regular writing will help keep those 'muscles' toned, so you can attack the final exams in peak condition.

Agility

Faced with a demanding or hard-to-understand question, there may be times when you'll find it handy to perform some mental gymnastics. Essay questions ask you to write about a topic from a *prescribed perspective*: that is, from a particular viewpoint, which you may or may not be familiar with, or feel comfortable with. Again, experience and practice will help you out with this. In general it is good to be flexible, ready to respond to whatever challenge you meet.

Particular skills

Essay writing brings together many separate skills, which we begin to build up in Chapter 4.

Pitfalls and false turns

Like climbing, writing can involve frustrating setbacks along the way: unexpected deadends, obstacles, twists in the path, cliffs that are too sheer. That's one reason to prepare in advance, rather than relying on the 'last night special', when it's too late to discover that you need additional information, or extra time to think, and so on.

Your studies in English and other subjects provide you with an opportunity to explore the world: to become aware of important issues in the modern world, to learn about great events in history, the lives of people in other places and other times, and the future that is emerging. The quality of your exploration and the enjoyment that you get out of it depend on you, your approach and your attitudes. You might as well make the most of it!

Chapter 2

About writing

- You *can* write!
- You can *learn* to write!
- Writing means rewriting.
- The stages of writing:

    'Garble'

    'Clarify'

    'Edit'

You *can* write!

Students often tell me: 'I know what I'm trying to say but I just can't write it' or, 'I just can't get my thoughts out onto paper'. Once they realise that words don't have to come out perfectly in the first draft, they usually start to make progress. Bad early experiences at home or school can cause poor self-esteem in very capable students.

No-one is a 'born' essay writer. The skill is like any other — acquired through practice and guidance. Those who take to it more quickly have usually done a lot of reading and writing already.

> Your ability to express ideas and to develop them will grow as you master the essay form.

Anyone who can speak English uses language. And anyone who can use language can write.

Many English students complain that they find it impossible to find the 'right' answer. However, what you are required to do is develop your own. This takes confidence, and the systematic approach described in Chapter 7 will help you gain this.

You can *learn* to write!

It is not, as some people say, 'impossible to learn essay writing'. On the other hand, it's not as easy as some people say either. I've seen impatient people exclaiming: 'Look. You just write an introduction, follow it up with the body and finish with a conclusion, right? That's all there is to it'.

That sounds easy enough. It's just as easy to build a house too — just lay foundations, put up a frame, lay a roof on it, then fill up the walls and windows. Simple — we can all build houses now can't we?

Obviously there are many other skills involved: the full job involves bricklaying, plumbing, sawing, draughting, an understanding of structural design ... Actually, essay writing starts to look pretty easy compared to housebuilding, but there are still a few 'tricks of the trade' you should try to master first! That's why we 'build up' to essay writing in this book by looking at basic skills first.

Writing means rewriting

- The essay is like a par 3–4 golf hole: it will usually take three to four 'strokes' — that is, drafts, to reach the goal. Even very experienced professional writers produce several drafts before the finished product is achieved.

- If an essay takes several drafts, how can I be expected to produce a good essay in forty minutes in the exam room? Good question. Go straight to Chapter 9, if you can't wait to find out the answer!

It is a common saying that 'Writing means rewriting'. We often think that because a published, finished piece of writing seems flawless, the writer producing it was infallible. However, a finished product will have taken much rewriting: usually several drafts at least. Quite possibly the first drafts would be unrecognisable as the source of the final product.

You can write. You'll never know that until you do it.

The stages of writing

The writing *process* involves a series of stages. At the start of my essay-writing workshops, I always ask people their aims. The only person I've ever told I couldn't help, wanted to learn to 'get it right first off'. He stayed on anyway and ended up happy enough to learn how to write like the rest of us mortals.

Depending on the stage of an essay, we tend to write in different ways:

1 The pre-writing stage

The pre-writing stage is the time between being given the question, and actually starting to draft the essay. This includes organising your thoughts, reading and taking notes, 'incubating', and starting to plan your essay. ('Incubating' means letting your ideas 'hatch' over a few days or so.)

Essays must always be relevant, but there are many different ways of answering a question; at the pre-writing stage, you plan how to answer the question. In the HSC you will often encounter essay questions that indicate in some way how to structure your answer. Many students assume there is only one 'right' way to answer any essay question.

The pre-writing stage is more problematic in English, however, for while you get plenty of opportunity for individual, independent thought, sometimes you are given few specific guidelines for your answer. Fortunately there are ways of preparing for this, (see Chapter 7). In English it is inevitable that you will come up with a different answer to others, because of a range of factors that can influence you, including:

- the way you interpret the question;
- different shades of understanding of key terms;
- your own background knowledge;
- whether you agree with a statement, or not;
- what weight you give to different aspects of the question;
- additional materials you have found yourself;
- the connections you make between prescribed texts, other readings and sources.

Some people call pre-writing the 'chaos' stage, since there is such a jumble of facts, thoughts, reference books, critical guides, interpretations, personal opinions and other sources available that you can get information overload, or find it hard to 'find the forest for the trees'. Since you can't cover every single aspect of a topic, you must narrow it down: on what angle, aspect or theme should you concentrate?

As you will see later, in most cases you can take particular guidance from the essay question itself.

2 First sketches and drafts

There are many reasons for finding it hard to 'get it out onto paper': apart from not being completely sure what you're trying to say, it could be nervousness, lack of self-esteem, being too hard on yourself, or telling yourself 'that's no good' or 'it'll never work' or 'that's not the right answer'. Maybe other people have given you a hard time in the past, and now you keep doing the same to yourself!

Remind yourself that the first draft is always a bit of a 'garble'. It's an experiment: feel free to push out those half-formed thoughts and vague ideas and don't worry about the words used to express them yet. No-one but you has to see your first drafts, so you are free to experiment.

In fact, many people have to get that 'garble' out of the way first; you can't start climbing the mountain from half-way up. The novelist Evelyn Waugh (*The Loved One*, *Brideshead Revisited* and many more), when asked the secret of his style, replied something like this: 'It's simple. First I get all the words out, then I push them around a little'. In a second draft you start to 'push the words around' to make more sense.

Planning even your first draft is preferable, but even some very experienced essay writers find they can't make a plan until after that, so the 'garble' draft provides a 'plan' for the second. If necessary, write your first draft in the spirit of brainstorming. No doubt you have used this technique elsewhere: usually in a group, everyone contributes their ideas, and all ideas are recorded without criticism, no matter how ridiculous. The whole point is to produce as many ideas as possible.

The first draft is often the hardest step to take, so don't inhibit yourself by being too self-critical. Later on, you will reread and decide which parts to use and which not. Tell yourself you are 'prospecting' or mining for ideas, and you will come up with some valuable material among the unusable stuff. The more material you dig up, the better the chance of finding something worthwhile, and it's far better to have too much than nothing to choose from.

3 Focusing

Once those first ideas are expressed, rewriting is a series of clarifications: making your ideas clearer, and more clearly expressed, by degrees — refining your 'ore'. As you sort through all the dirt and rock you've dug up, you should find some gold. Of course it doesn't emerge shining and whole from the ground, but in an imperfect state, so you need to refine it and shape it appropriately.

Reading back over what you have written, focus on the strongest points and build your essay on them.

4 Redefining/refocusing

You may find that the draft essay needs change of some sort: perhaps you've left out important points. You may need further research, or to reread your textbooks. You may have included discussion of facts that are irrelevant, and should be taken out. The focus of attention may need to be broadened or narrowed, or perhaps you haven't answered the question properly.

Sometimes (particularly with English again) what you originally wanted to say is different from, or even the reverse of, what you now consider the best answer. That's okay: writing essays is a learning process, and deliberately adopting an attitude of openness, of 'discovery' through writing, will help free you up for this.

When redefining, you check the facts, the logic and conclusions of your draft essay. Check definitions of keywords and any other areas you're not certain of.

5 Editing

The final stages of clarification and refining are the 'editing' stages. Editing means several things, but a handy working definition would be 'to prepare a piece of writing to be read by the public'. In other words, to check your essay over to make it as professional and polished as possible.

Editing operates on two levels, the 'macro' and 'micro' levels. *Macro-editing* looks at the 'big picture', particularly the structure of the essay, answering the question, and the discussion of points. Is there a clear introduction and conclusion? Are the main points ordered in a logical way? Does the conclusion refer to the main points raised in the introduction? Are any important details missing? Are some of the matters discussed irrelevant to the question? Has paragraphing been used correctly throughout?

Micro-editing looks at the finer details such as grammar, spelling and punctuation, and most of this is done at the final draft stage, polishing the essay before it is handed up. Imprecise use of language can obscure the intended meaning of your words, or even alter it. One student wrote that 'People who are both women and men play pool'. What he meant to say was that men and women play pool; what he actually said, would make us wonder about the gender of the pool players!

A 'word perfect' presentation is certainly impressive in all subjects, and is a definite asset for English assignments. However, you shouldn't worry about the finer points until editing the final draft. Don't worry about spelling and grammar too much until then. Ideas, structure and facts must come first. Don't bother polishing the sculpture until the shape is complete! In the words of the great satirist Jonathan Swift:

> When a Man's Thoughts are clear, the properest Words will generally offer themselves first; and his own Judgement will direct him in what Order to place them, so as they may be best understood.

(And speaking of micro-editing, these days the word 'properest' would be changed to 'most proper', nor do we use 'Man' to stand for 'people' in general, since this is considered sexist.)

A word of warning; don't go overboard with editing. Writers can get rather neurotic and find it hard to let go of a work. I once attended a reading by a well-known Canadian author. When a student asked her at what stage she knew her manuscript was finished, she replied that she had been changing the words even as she read! There comes a point when you simply have to decide that the work is finished.

Chapter 3

The good essay

What an essay isn't

Let's start with a story. It's your 17th birthday and your parents have promised that if you study hard at school they will buy you a second-hand car (this is called 'bribery'). You get up in a hurry that morning. The parents' car is parked in the driveway and you know that SOMETHING has been locked up inside the garage. You beg Mum for the key and with a smile she gives it to you. Heart pounding, you push open the door, switch on the light and see:

What is it? It's … a pile of junk. Greasy engine cogs, springs, axleshafts, body panels; there's a steering wheel … you pick it up in a state of shock and stare at the thing in disbelief. You can't help yourself; you call out 'What's this?' The parents come up behind you and when you turn around, suddenly there they are beaming proudly. You fight back the tears.

'Do you like it?' Dad asks.

'What is it?'

'A sportscar of course! Good eh?'

It certainly doesn't look it.

A junk heap

'Yes', Dad says proudly. 'It's a Triumph. Needs a little work of course, but it's all there. A real goer. Happy birthday.' Gee thanks Mum and Dad. They try hard.

I once had a private student studying a Topic Area ('The Future'), similar to the Special Area of Study now common to Standard and Advanced English. Diana was trying to study for the Trials. She was bright and articulate, an excellent public speaker, but told me she was 'failing' English in most assessments and couldn't seem to write an essay.

I asked her: what do you think about this topic? What do you think about The Future?

'I don't know'.

'What do you *think* about it?'

'I've got some notes in a folder …' Before I could stop her she flopped the folder on the desk. 'Before you open that' I said, 'What do you *think* about The Future? What's in those notes?' She said 'I don't know. Can't remember.'

'What you've got there is a pile of junk.'

She looked at me — anger starting to show in her face.

Untogether

Diana had told me she was finding it hard to collect supplementary materials on this subject. That surprised me — there is so much on this topic in the newspapers every week.

I said 'Why? What are you looking for?'

'I don't know' she said.

That's why.

The junkpile of car parts, the pile of useless notes, the inability to find the right information: all have something in common. Or rather, they lack something in common. What they lack is structure, and without structure, little can be achieved.

Sure, the car's all there. It's just up to you to put it together the right way. Sure, the notes and clippings could be useful too — but have you ever tried to solve a jigsaw puzzle without a photograph of the picture in front of you? It's a lot harder, isn't it. Ever tried finding something when you don't know what you're looking for? That's hard too.

Teachers and overworked HSC markers don't like to have to sift through random piles of words, trying to piece together what the student's trying to say; it's your job to put it together for them.

What an essay is

> ▌ An essay without an argument and an organised structure is a 'pile of junk'. SORRY!

It might help to imagine you are the Crown Prosecutor in a murder trial. The charge against the defendant is read out and you're called to present your case. You have researched the matter carefully: gathered lots of evidence, read and reread the relevant sections of the law, and put together a case to convince judge and jury that the charge is correct.

At least, you'd better have: for in a court of law the onus of proof lies on you. Just like an essay, you must not only present all the relevant information, but also show how it 'proves' your case, by means of an **argument**: a line of discussion. And any irrelevancies will only make the 'judge' cranky.

■ The purpose of an essay is to establish a 'case' and prove it as fully and convincingly as possible.

Essays are monumentally difficult; that's the general opinion. Let's just demolish that belief with a shatteringly simple answer:

■ The essay is nothing but ideas, supported by evidence.

Before I explain this further, let's look at some different ways people have tried to write essays.

1 You have something to say. You state it. You don't know what else to write. So you just keep writing anything and hope no-one notices. Essays are just all waffle anyway! *Or*:

2 You write every single thing you know about a subject: lots of details. Good; that should do it. Oh, and at the end, stick in a bit of a conclusion. *Or*:

3 You get blinding flashes of inspiration, write off a lengthy draft in an hour or so, and go off to sleep. Next day when you reread it, it's gibberish.

There are lots of other variations too, but let's stick with these three 'recipes'. The first is the 'tubular spaghetti' style of essay. It twirls around in circles, just repeating itself. It's not 'going anywhere', and it's hollow.

The second is not hollow, and it's going plenty of places. All over the place in fact; nothing is keeping it together. Fair enough for an Irish stew, but not a good recipe for essays.

The third is even messier of course, virtually alphabet soup. But it does have something important: it has an idea, maybe a few. It's trying to say something, even if the words are garbled. You can probably use the ideas to build an essay. This chapter has one main idea that I'm trying to communicate: that the essay is nothing but *ideas*, supported by *evidence*. I have made an assertion: in the following discussion I will back it up with evidence.

A definition

Various definitions of 'essay' are given in dictionaries. Two lesser-known meanings describe essays as 'experiments', or as a kind of 'judgement'. *Chambers' Twentieth Century Dictionary* calls it 'an attempt: a tentative effort', a 'first draft', a 'trial' or 'experiment'. The word originally meant 'to weigh', and 'to try, examine'. Essays often do 'weigh' up the evidence for and against a proposition or idea, balance the arguments and come up with a detailed assessment.

Here's a useful definition:

> An essay is a *sustained argument* developing or weighing the evidence about an idea or question, and creating a *full* and satisfying *conclusion*.

There are three key elements to this — let's look at each of them in turn.

Sustained

It's no use for a defeated marathon runner to claim victory because she was fastest in the first hundred metres. Nor can your essay come up with a quick answer and leave it at that: 'sustained' means that you keep it going. When I was in Year 11 the head teacher of English used to write at the end of my essays: 'You must write more'. My reaction was, 'Why? I've said all I wanted to in a few paragraphs, so why pad it all out into several pages?' I couldn't see the point in wasting paper and ink.

What did the teacher really mean? (If only he'd written a more complete answer himself, I wouldn't have had to work it out for myself, much later!)

> The ability to write a good essay is a skill that is as important as your knowledge and ideas themselves.

Anybody can respond randomly to a 'multiple guess' test and have about one in four chances of getting the right answer. But to be able to write a whole, cohesive essay shows that you have a genuine understanding of your topic, as well as the ability to express it. Essays aren't merely about 'giving the right answer' but about demonstrating the depth and extent of your understanding and knowledge, your ability to reason, to argue an opinion, to make judgements, to analyse, to express yourself in written language fluently, and to employ appropriate terminology. Writing 'more', does *not* mean 'padding' an essay with repetition or irrelevant details, 'telling the story' or using random quotes, etc. 'Padding' is extremely easy to spot, and most unimpressive to the marker!

Argument (line of discussion)

Forget your usual understanding of the word 'argument': the essay isn't a quarrel or fight but an opinion, a proposition, an idea, a theme or the disclosure of information. The word 'argument' is used in this book to mean your main line of discussion, the theme you are developing. Arguments are the backbone of the essay.

An essay, like a tree, can grow from one simple source. A tree can begin with one seed. This germinates and sprouts, sending the first shoots out into the light of day. Properly nurtured, with appropriate nutrients and conditions, that thin stem will eventually grow into a tall, thick trunk.

Your essay can grow on paper, under the study lamp, from one single idea — your argument or theme — and should develop in a straight line from start to finish (otherwise it has problems).

The analogy can be extended further: a tree can be very complex, having many branches, sub-branches, leaves, etc. It may flower, fruit, and even harbour various inhabitants! But always that main structure is there. Likewise, your argument may branch off into various topics, but these must be linked somehow to the argument (otherwise they'll fall off!). Of course, these branches can have sub-branches and small details themselves.

Full conclusion

In the best essays, conclusions 'bear fruit': they go beyond a mere summary of the discussion and look at the implications and significance more fully.

There's our definition of the essay: it's not merely an idea, but one line of discussion supported by information and knowledge, pruned and nurtured by your writing and editing skills. The best essays cap off the discussion with some sense of 'something extra': what the discussion leads us to conclude, the implications of what we have written. (*Note*: the conclusion should not, however, introduce new material.)

The good essay

What makes a good essay? The good essay is:

- relevant
- complete
- cohesive
- sustained
- well-organised
- concise
- 'signposted'
- specific
- explanatory

- analytical/critical
- fluently expressed.

Each of these terms is now explained briefly. In Chapter 4 they are treated in more detail and exercises are given to help you practise relevant skills.

Relevant

Answer the question! It is *not* good enough to write just anything about the general subject; you must meet the specific requirements. This shouldn't need to be said at all, but an overwhelming number of teachers agree: one of the most common errors made by students is simply not answering the question. There are a number of possible ways this could happen:

- You can't understand the question.
- You can't analyse the question.
- You don't have any answer.
- You don't know much about the topic.
- You haven't bothered to try!

If your problem is either of the first two, help is at hand in Chapter 4. The more experience you get with answering questions, the better you'll become at understanding them and learning to know the kinds of questions to expect. If it's either of the next two, you need to work on your study. If your problem is the last alternative, I must emphasise that it is far less 'bother' to consider the question from the start than to go off on a detour and have to start all over again later!

OPEN QUESTIONS AND CLOSED QUESTIONS

Essay questions can offer a varied scope of response, from 'open' to 'closed'. The *open* question is broad and allows many options in your answer. A good example of an open type is this HSC English question:

> How have the texts you have studied this year effectively shaped your understanding of the meaning of 'change'? In your answer you should refer to your prescribed text, ONE text from the prescribed stimulus booklet *Changing*, and a variety of other related texts of your own choosing.
>
> (Board of Studies 2001 Higher School Certificate Specimen Examination Paper, English (Standard) and (Advanced))

This question does specify the theme of change, but otherwise allows you a free hand in deciding what aspects to discuss, so long as you refer to the variety of texts they stipulate and answer how these texts have 'effectively shaped' your understanding.

Open questions give you much freedom, and for students who are well prepared, they can be a godsend. On the other hand, they may give you little direction, and that is why many students flounder on such questions; unable to think of anything, not knowing where to start.

Many students believe that a *closed* question is easier because it 'tells you what to do'. It specifies more narrowly the aspects of a topic on which you should focus. A closed question on a novel might ask you to discuss the relationship of two main characters, a particular incident in relation to the whole story, a quote or a particular theme. Here is an example of a 'closed' essay question:

> Australia is a limited market. Businesses situated in such markets seek global remedies. Critically examine how the Australian market is limiting the growth of a business you have studied and the consequences for two different stakeholders when this business expands into the global marketplace.
>
> (Board of Studies, 2001 HSC Specimen Examination Paper, Business Studies.)

The above question requires you to understand what is meant by a 'limited market', to know about 'global remedies', how the Australian market has limited the growth of some business you have studied, and the consequences of global expansion.

Both kinds of question have their pros and cons. The freedom of the 'open' question must be met with your own initiative, but at least it gives you more scope to write about what interests you, or what you have studied and thought about most closely. While the closed question does signpost the way for you, it could be a way with which you're not very familiar: a technical aspect of theatre, film or multimedia, a minor character, an unexpected theme or aspect, or something you've simply overlooked or ignored.

Either way, you still have to make sure to answer the question!

Complete

'Complete' doesn't mean long, nor filled with irrelevant details. It certainly doesn't mean 'containing every single fact you know about the topic' either. A complete essay has an argument, discussion of a number of points relating to that, and a conclusion tying the points together. It doesn't assume that the reader already knows what s/he needs to know; the complete essay discusses all that is necessary to establish your point and includes all the logical steps to build up the whole picture.

Cohesive

'Cohesive' means that it 'hangs together'. What we are reading isn't a random set of facts, or just a pile of words, but points with a definite purpose in common.

Sustained

This purpose is *sustained* throughout the essay.

Well-organised

A well-organised essay is structured so that related points are grouped together and so that there's a logic to their sequence (that is, we can see how each point leads to the next). A well-organised essay introduces the main points early and then treats each of them in turn, according to some logical order.

Concise (and clear)

Don't be unnecessarily wordy. Your meaning is often clearer when it's expressed in fewer words. Some students will take four or five lines to express an idea that needs only two.

Signposted

It is very annoying to read some interesting discussion, and yet be unable to see what the writer is actually getting at. You can 'show the way' to a reader by:

- announcing your points in advance;
- using linking words and phrases;
- showing how your points relate to the main theme;
- using sequence, such as 'first', 'secondly', etc.

Specific

It is always impressive to see that a writer is closely engaged with the subject material: it is advisable to quote relevant details about events or theories and to use the appropriate technical terminology or specialised vocabulary in support of your argument. In English, a specific essay will discuss significant characters or scenes in detail. In Economics, quote financial events, policy changes, and statistics, etc.

You may know a lot about a subject, but if you don't get specific, you haven't 'proved' this, and you've undersold yourself. Your reader is not a mindreader!

Explanatory

It's one thing to know your facts, and another to be able to explain their significance — obviously it is preferable to 'prove' your case by making explicit links between facts you introduce, and your argument.

Advanced essay skills

Analysis

An average student might take ideas found in books for granted, at their 'face value'. Better-than-average students look deeper.

Fluency

In English in particular, the top-banded essays are very well expressed. This takes practice!

sectiontwo:

Building essays

Chapter 4

Training workouts:
the microskills

Analysing the question: relevance

What is the question really about? What is it asking you to do? Analysing the question is crucial: it's rather tragic for students who hand up a fine essay on the right subject, only to discover that they didn't answer the question. This goes down very poorly with teachers and examiners! One way of making sure you're 'on track' is to note carefully the keywords.

Find keywords

Keywords are the clues in a question that specify the subject you are to discuss, refer you to a particular aspect of it, and tell you what to do in your discussion.

- *Subject* keywords tell you what text or broad area of study you are to discuss. These are often specified in a heading above the question itself in HSC papers, but may not be in class essays. (You are not likely to get this wrong, most of the time!)

- *Topic* keywords specify what part of the subject you should discuss.

- *Aspect* keywords specify that particular parts of that topic be considered.

- '*Doing*' keywords specify what you are asked to 'do', for example: 'explain', 'discuss', 'compare', etc.

<u>Discuss</u> a range of strategies that could be used by employers in the <u>business services industry</u> to raise employee <u>awareness of issues</u> relating to <u>occupational health and safety</u>.

(Board of Studies 2001 HSC Specimen Examination Paper, Business Services — Office Administration.)

In the above question, the broad *subject* is the business services industry. The specific focus or *topic* is occupational health and safety. The *aspect* of that focus you are asked about is strategies to raise employee awareness, and the '*doing*' keyword is to 'discuss'.

Any question will have keywords, although you may not find all four types. For example, a question may specify a broad topic related to the subject, but leave the choice of particular aspects up to you.

EXERCISES

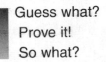

1 Look up old exam papers in the subjects you are studying, and find the keywords in essay questions.

2 Decide the type of each keyword.

The 3-step structure: completeness

The essay has a simple 1-2-3 structure. A similar pattern can also be used in a paragraph. It's excellent practice, a kind of 'micro-essay'.

In one paragraph, we can announce a 'case', support it and then cap it off in some way. I use three simple terms to help remind me of what I'm trying to achieve:

> Guess what?
> Prove it!
> So what?

- *Guess what?* — What am I trying to say, establish, describe or prove? This is stated in a topic sentence. (We look at topic sentences in the next section. They form the backbone of the paragraph, just as the argument is the backbone of an essay.)

- *Prove it!* — How can I back it up?

- *So what?* — Try to 'make something of it'. Relate this to my main argument, or cap off the point I'm making here.

EXERCISE

E

Read the following paragraph carefully and relate each section to the above steps.

> 1. Energy conservation is an environmental issue with implications for everyday life. 2. In their own homes, people have the choice to reduce their energy consumption by various means: by cutting down on unnecessary energy consumption, by installing insulation, by designing energy-efficient homes such as 'solar passive', and by using 'green' energy sources such as solar energy. 3. Not to conserve energy in the household is to choose not to care about the environment.

Now read the following three paragraphs and decide whether or not they follow this pattern. Where does each step begin?

(a) The poems of Bruce Dawe are preoccupied with the suburban life of Australia. In particular, 'Enter without so much as knocking', 'Homo Suburbiensis', 'Life cycle' and 'And a Good Friday was had by all' treat various aspects of suburban life, such as the corrupting influence of consumerism, the meaningless chatter of the commercial media, the snatches of trivial conversation. However, not all is lost: in 'Homo Suburbiensis' the gardener has found in his suburban patch an oasis of quiet in which to contemplate the timeless issues of 'pain, love, hate, age, war, death, laughter, fever.'

(b) In this essay I will outline some of the areas that have benefited from changing values and norms in relation to the family, focusing on Australian families. First I will look at the functions performed by the family, and how the structure of the family has evolved from an extended kin family to an isolated nuclear family. Then I will look at the changes in reasons for marriage and the reasons for staying married, showing that now romantic love is the motivation for marriage, as opposed to economic benefit. Finally I will outline how many of the changes in values and norms in relation to the family have benefited women and children.

(c) Writing is a craft, and like many crafts it requires a variety of skills. The leather worker may need a steady hand, a straight eye, and an appreciation of quality materials, as well as a creative flair for embossing designs and choosing appropriate buckles, etc. The essay writer must develop a variety of skills too: these include efficient study or research, clear thinking, the ability to use an appropriate form, and the ability to use language persuasively and correctly. The isolation of these particular skills also makes it possible to identify and work on individual areas of weakness.

ANSWER TO EXERCISE

(a) Yes.

    1 'The poems of ...'

    2 'In particular, ...'

    3 'Not all is lost ...'

(b) No.

    1 'In this essay I will ...'

    2 'First I will look ...'

(This is obviously an introductory paragraph, and a final 'cap' is not required here.)

(c) Yes.

    1 'Writing is a craft ...'

      '... requires a variety of skills ...'

    2 'The leather worker ...'

      'The essay writer ...'

    3 'The isolation of ...'

(This is a more complicated example because it is 'double-barrelled': the writer is making a comparison throughout, between crafts and writing.)

Completeness in short-response answers

I had a student who asked me why he only got half a mark out of two for a reading passage question. The question asked something like 'How does the writer feel?', and John had written: 'She feels sad'. 'That's right isn't it?' he asked.

Yes, it was right. But those few words weren't worth two marks. A complete answer will tell us quite a bit more than he did. The reading passage was a newspaper feature article written by a mother, about her daughter leaving home. We can follow the 1-2-3 pattern:

■ *Guess what?* — The mother is sad.

The next step is to 'Prove it'. A relevant quote will help.

■ *Prove it* — 'The page is swimming before her eyes.': in other words, she's crying.

Now we can cap this off in some way. The obvious way would be to explain why she's sad.

■ *So what?* — 'She's crying because just when her daughter's old enough to be her friend, she's losing her to the daughter's own friends.'

EXERCISES

E

Write complete paragraphs using the '3-step pattern', starting with the following:

(1) There are many reasons for introducing daylight saving.

(2) It's wrong to say that essay-writing skills are important; they are essential!

(3) Before criticising his friend's faults, he should have looked at his own first.

(4) There are many exciting things to do on Slipstream Island.

(5) It was a perfect day.

Topic sentences: cohesive

A very common, and important student weakness is the lack of topic sentences. Topic sentences:

■ give shape and purpose to your writing;

■ help create order within the paragraph;

■ allow the reader to follow the argument;

■ demonstrate an understanding of formal writing.

The topic sentence often, but not always, begins the paragraph and states or introduces the *theme* of that paragraph, or the point it's making. (However, it will sometimes appear at the end of a paragraph, and sometimes in the middle. There is no rule about this.) To start a paragraph with a topic sentence is to start with a purpose, and while it gives the paragraph unity and order, it also gives power to your writing by focusing it.

If you are asked to write a paragraph about the characters in a particular drama or novel, it's human nature to start just listing them in no particular order, briefly describing them according to whatever ideas first came to mind. Writing a topic sentence 'up front' will help convert 'junk' into building blocks.

About Peter Skrzynecki's poem 'Migrant Hostel' you could say that:

> The poem describes the migrants as birds, or like imprisoned criminals, or like helpless dumb creatures.

These points may be correct, but the sentence reads like an unconvincing list of ideas, which doesn't really tell us much. The following paragraph develops one idea, stated in a topic sentence at the start:

> Stanza by stanza, Skrzynecki builds up an image of helpless, caged birds. Initially described as people who can't keep track of what's going on, the migrants are then compared to a homing pigeon 'circling to get its bearings'. These birds, however, aren't really 'homing' because they have left home, and in the third stanza they are more like 'birds of passage' but without the freedom to follow the seasons at their will. Finally, the barricading arm of the migrant hostel completes the effect of their being imprisoned; these people's lives are either effectively behind them now, or they are helplessly waiting for their life to begin.

In the above paragraph, the strongest idea has been selected and the rest of the paragraph develops the idea stated in the topic sentence.

Topic sentences make your writing easier to read and your argument easier to follow. More importantly, they ensure that you are clear about what *you* are trying to say. As an exercise, make a point when revising your essays of highlighting the topic sentence in each paragraph. If you can't find one, write one for it. (This may also involve reshaping the entire paragraph, and your work will be stronger for the extra effort.)

Recognising topic sentences

Read the following paragraphs and decide whether they have topic sentences or not. If so, underline them.

1 When I arrived at university I found that I could no longer expect everyone and everything to change for my sake. In fact, it was me who had to change. Not everyone agreed with my opinions in tutorials. Not everyone felt I was an outstanding fount of wisdom. From being a class leader at school, I was now just one of the group, no more special than anyone else.

2 You can go to the beach, or for a long hike in the bush. How about a long bike ride, or hiring a tennis court for the afternoon with a group of friends? Then there are less energetic activities too: why not catch a new movie or visit the art gallery? Learn a new craft, or how to play an instrument? There are always plenty of things to do in your holidays.

3 Opinions about Madonna are divided. Some women feel that she has been a very positive symbol of female pride and strength, since she projects such a confident, self-assured image and seems to know exactly what she wants and how to get it. Others complain that her emphasis on body image and fashion just reinforces the old male myth that women are just sex objects.

4 *The Club* is a drama about the politics of an Aussie Rules football club, but really this could be the story of any sporting organisation. An old club tradition is betrayed by 'buying' the star player Geoff Hayward. Jock, the club's administrator pretends to be a father figure to Geoff but then betrays his confidence. And the coach Laurie is betrayed by the entire club, although they feel he betrayed them by making comments to the media.

ANSWERS

1 First sentence.

2 Last sentence.

3 First sentence.

4 Trick: the first sentence appears to be a topic sentence, yet close reading shows that the student hasn't actually written about this topic at all. A better topic sentence would focus on 'betrayal' as a theme.

Composing topic sentences

Here is a series of paragraphs, with the topic sentences removed. Try to make up a topic sentence to go with them.

1 ... If you don't have a passport, you must apply for one well in advance of your departure. Many countries require an entry visa. Travel insurance is also considered an absolute necessity. And if you are planning to drive overseas, you must apply for an international driving permit in some countries.

2 There will be women reading this book who may well be saying to themselves, 'This is all very well and good, but it's hardly of interest to me. What chance do I have of ever becoming Prime Minister?' The answer is that your chances are better than you think and a lot better than they would have been twenty or even ten years ago ... As the following tables will show, the number of women MPs is increasing annually. The more female MPs there are, the more chance there is of one of them getting into The Lodge. Where once there was a reluctance by political parties to endorse women as candidates, there is now keen competition between parties to have the most women in the various parliaments.

(Barry Cohen, *How to Become Prime Minister*, Penguin, 1990, p. 76.)

3 ... They sing in the air, buzz in the classrooms, wail in streets, murmur in bedrooms. They shape daily lives and nightly fears. Wars are begun on the strength of a good story and could not be started without one. If a people's stories are destroyed they wander dispossessed on the fringes of others' stories, and eventually dissolve into oblivion. Journeys are begun, colonies are founded, hearts are broken, souls inspired. If you're not in a story, you don't exist ...

(Patti Miller, *The Last One Who Remembers*, Allen and Unwin, 1997, p.17.)

4 There are no prizes for getting it right. There was no moment when, for the first time, Australia was seen 'as it really was' ... A national identity is an invention. There is no point asking whether one version of this essential Australia is truer than another because they are all intellectual constructs, neat, tidy, comprehensible — and necessarily false. They have all been artificially imposed upon a diverse landscape and population, and a variety of untidy social relationships, attitudes and emotions.

(Richard White, *Inventing Australia*, Allen and Unwin, 1981, p. viii.)

Your topic sentences should state something like the following:

1 There is much preparation required before travelling overseas.

2 Women's chances of becoming the Australian Prime Minister are getting better and better. (This is a very *cohesive* paragraph.)

3 Story is all-important.

4 There is no single, 'true' Australian identity.

Paragraphing: sustained

Paragraphing is not such a difficult skill, but it is an important one. Dividing up your writing into paragraphs shows that you are organised, and makes an essay easier to read. When we read an essay we want to see how the argument is progressing from one point to the next.

Unlike this book, and unlike reports, essays don't use headings. This makes them look less 'reader friendly', so it is important to use paragraphs regularly, to break up the mass of words and to signal the making of a new point. It also tends to put the marker in a good mood! An unparagraphed page gives the reader the feeling of hacking a way through thick jungle without a track in sight — not very enjoyable, and very hard work. A neat series of paragraphs acts like stepping stones that can be followed pleasurably across the river.

Most students find the process of deciding where to begin and end paragraphs reasonably easy; you will soon get a 'feel' for it with a little practice. Obviously, whenever you write a topic sentence, this may be a good place to start a new paragraph.

Paragraph unity

If topic sentences remind us to 'keep to the point', paragraphing reminds us to separate point from point, to show where one topic ends and the next begins. 'Paragraph unity' means that each paragraph deals with one main idea only. Once that point has been made and supported, move on to a new paragraph.

The topic sentence of each paragraph should propel your argument by advancing the next logical step and showing how it relates. For example, a student writing an essay about factors affecting employment patterns in Australia treated four factors:

(a) the economic climate (boom or bust?);

(b) industry restructuring;

(c) privatisation and corporatisation of industries;

(d) technological innovation.

She treated each of these points for a couple of paragraphs or so. The topic sentences introducing each point began like this:

(a) Traditionally, the level of growth and activity of the Australian economy has been considered the chief factor affecting employment ...

(b) However, with major changes in regulatory frameworks, another important factor in Australian employment patterns in recent years has been the major changes brought about by industry restructuring ...

(c) Another factor affecting these patterns in recent times has been the trend to privatisation or corporatisation of functions formerly undertaken by government agencies, such as ...

(d) The climate of rapid and widespread technological innovation has also had a dramatic effect on employment patterns ...

Note that each sentence introduces the new point, as well as reminding us of the main topic. This keeps the argument *sustained* throughout the essay.

How long should a paragraph be? There is no ideal or 'correct' length for paragraphs, although the preference is for shorter rather than longer ones. As a rough guide, consider 6–7 word-processed or handwritten foolscap lines a fair aim; half a page is certainly too long; three lines usually too short! The most important thing is simply to use paragraphing.

Indenting

Many teachers still prefer you to indent the start of a paragraph: that is, to start your paragraph about one tab stop to the right of the margin, or roughly one centimetre on a handwritten page. If you do start paragraphs 'flush left', that is, at the margin, like the rest of your lines, you must leave a line space between each paragraph to signal the start of a new paragraph. Check with your teacher what she or he prefers!

1 Read the following extract, which has been retyped without paragraphing.
   Decide where paragraphs should go.

In the beginning was the pun

... Puns have always been known, and some have achieved great
fame — notably the *Peter/rock* play on words in the New Testament
(clearer in French, where *pierre* is used for both), or the puns used
by the oracle at Delphi (such as the ambiguous reply to the general
who wished to know whether he should go on a journey: *Domine,
stes* vs *Domin ne stes*, 'Master, stay' vs 'At home do not stay'.
Shakespeare was one of the greatest users of puns. In France, one of
the most famous punsters was the Marquis de Bièvre, in whose
never-acted play *Vercingètorix* there is an italicised pun in every line.
Puns are a feature of many linguistic contexts, such as black
comedy, sick humour, T-shirts, lapel badges, car stickers, trade
names, book titles, and graffiti. The world of advertising makes great
use of the economical impact and freshness of a pun (e.g. the slogan
for a new kind of adhesive, 'Our word is your bond'). But the best
and worst of them are found in everyday conversation. Puns that
have been justly lauded include the response of the disappointed
recipient of poor quality flowers ('With fronds like these who needs
anemones?'), the comment made by the circus manager to the
human cannonball who wanted to leave ('Where will I find another
man of your calibre?'), and the comment about the Spanish girls in
a certain town, that they are 'senoreaters'. Puns have been called
verbal practical jokes, and are either loved or hated according to
temperament. Their popularity varies greatly between languages and
cultures, though the reasons for this are unclear; it has been said, for
example, that they are far more popular in Britain than in the USA,
and in France than in Germany. But punning is not without its
dangers. The Gnat, in Lewis Carroll's *The Hunting of the Snark*, dies
of a pun. And punsters should beware the phenomenon of
compulsive punning, first recorded by a German surgeon in 1939,
and now known as 'Förster's syndrome'.

(From: *The Cambridge Encyclopaedia of Language*, by David Crystal, Cambridge
University Press, 1987, p. 63.)

ANSWERS

There are three paragraphs, based on three different topics introduced by the following topic sentences:

- … Puns have always been known, and some have achieved great fame …
- Puns are a feature of many linguistic contexts …
- Puns have been called verbal practical jokes …

Did you notice how hard it was to read when not paragraphed?

Organising data: well-organised

Writing is very slow and *linear*: it can only travel in a straight *line*, handling one idea, one direction at a time. So it is important to unravel your ideas one by one, in an organised way. If you don't do this, your reader will become confused.

Your essay needs several levels of organisation. First there is the overall Introduction–Body–Conclusion structure, which you know. Secondly, you need to order the topics discussed in the body, and thirdly, within each topic, related points should be organised too.

Consider that pile of car parts again. Each individual piece belongs with specific others, and together they make up a structure called an 'assembly'. For example, steering-related parts make up a steering-assembly, brake parts form a brake assembly, and so on.

Likewise, your information should be sorted into groups. This involves two main processes: *grouping* related points together, and *ranking* points within the group.

Grouping

Say you're writing an essay about *The Stolen Children: Their Stories*. Some perspectives to consider would include themes such as belonging, childhood trauma, and reconciliation. While taking notes for the essay, you would collect information under those headings. Taking notes and organising your ideas for an Ancient History question on historical methodology, you might use the headings of written evidence, archaeology and science.

Subgrouping

You can also use subgroups where appropriate, dividing groups into smaller groups. For example, you might want to discuss 'belonging' in *The Stolen Children* under three different subheadings: family belonging, belonging to a broader society with a different culture, and belonging in the future.

Ordering

It is important to discuss points in order. There are various ways of deciding how to arrange this, and you'll usually find that the particular essay you are writing will suggest how to do it. Different *ordering principles* are available to you:

- *Order of importance*: start with the most important or persuasive facts, then treat progressively less important ones. (*Or*: start with lesser points and work up to the most important ones.) An essay about the characters in Macbeth will probably concentrate on the main characters first: Duncan, Macbeth and Lady Macbeth, etc., unless the question asks you to focus on the lesser characters.

- *From central to less central*: broad view to specific. It is conventional to give the 'big picture' before treating details. For instance, the introduction should mention the main points to be treated, but not go into detail.

- *Chronological (time) order*: A history essay might discuss events and movements in the sequence in which they occurred in time.

- *Geography*: you could describe the terrain of a country, starting from west and working east, then from north to south, etc. You could describe a house starting from (say) the exterior, then moving to the interior, then going from room to room, starting from the front.

- *Cause–effect*: this is the idea that something caused an effect of some sort. To answer why Ted is led to resigning as Club President in David Williamson's play *The Club*, you need to trace the causes in the events preceding it. Sometimes there may be a *causal chain*, where a series of events is set off by some factor.

- *Comparison*: you can discuss all the positive aspects first, then the negative (or vice versa), e.g., the advantages and disadvantages of a government policy.

E

1 (a) Think about the English text you have read or viewed most recently. (N.B. a 'text' can include a film or multimedia production in the new syllabus.) Make a list of the characters according to three categories:

- Main characters

- Minor characters

- Incidental characters (people who only make a brief, passing appearance).

(b) Make a similar list of major, minor, and trivial incidents in that book.

2 (a) What is important to you in your life? Think of at least four categories of things that are important to you. Use these categories as headings and list five examples under each heading.

(b) For each category, give each of these five examples a number from 1 to 5, starting with the most important.

3 Look at the above list of organisational principles. Think of an essay topic where you might use each one. In which subjects might you use them? e.g., Modern History, Legal Studies, Earth and Environmental Science.

4 Think of a recent event. What was the cause (or causes), in your opinion? Make a list of everything that might have contributed to this happening. For example:

Causes of events in Ron's household that night

- Ron had a stressful day at work.

- He had to stay back late to fix an emergency problem, so missed his usual train home.

- He missed the last bus from the station, and had to walk.

- He hates being late.

- He arrived home very late, angry and tired.

- Ron snapped at his kids when they greeted him.

- Ron apologised to his kids.

Summarising: concise

Summarising is an essential skill, for the following reasons:

Getting the big picture

Before treating details, we first need to understand the overall situation. As we've discussed, it's hard to finish a jigsaw without knowing what the picture looks like. Most novels, for instance, will be composed of a number of characters and a series of events or other developments. *The Stolen Children* tells many different stories in one book, but we need to be able to discuss the book as a whole.

Simplifying your notes and ideas

Another word for summary is *précis*, and a good summary is both precise and concise since it decides what are the essential points, and what are the lesser, supporting points.

Articulating your ideas

Writing a summary makes you express your ideas on paper, to test and develop them. Often we believe we know what we feel about a film or book until we actually try to find words to express this. Students tend to assume that summarising is more or less 'automatic', and yet when asked to summarise an English text, they just start to 'tell the story' from the beginning, or to recount whatever they can remember.

That is not a 'summary', however. Some people can rattle off the entire story of a movie in vivid detail, scene by scene, yet are completely unable to encapsulate what it's 'all about', to give the gist of it quickly. That's what we do need: a general overview. Frequently we discover that we have to give the matter further thought. A short summary can be an excellent foundation for all further study in a topic, since it starts the process of clarifying your thoughts at an early stage.

Helping you remember

Summaries help to cement important ideas in your memory. The best way to remember things is to actively organise your thoughts in some way. It's an excellent idea to summarise a book or topic immediately after studying it, so that you don't forget most of it months later, as so many students do.

■ A summary gives you the 'big picture' in few words!

The idea of a summary is to reduce a complex set of information to a manageable whole. The length can vary, but you may discover that the smaller the summary, the harder it is to write. So this is a great exercise in concision. Try, for instance, to write a one-paragraph summary of the last book you have read. Here are some pointers:

Give the essential information: Who, what, where, when, how, and why. About Michael Gow's play *Away*, we could say that 'The drama is set in Australia in the summer holidays of 1967–68, and focuses on the problems and aspirations of three separate family groups.' We could go on to outline these separate problems and aspirations, probably starting with the sickness of Harry and Vic's son, Tom. It can take a little practice to see which points are essential and which aren't. The best test is to try to eliminate them: if the summary still makes sense, the detail isn't necessary.

Just as the essay is structured 1–2–3, and just as the paragraph and short response exam answer can follow this pattern, so can the summary.

Here is the beginning of a three-step summary of Bruce Dawe's poem 'Abandonment of Autos'. The first step is to sum up broadly. Secondly, we start to add detail.

1 This is a poem inspired by the attraction of freedom.

2 It focuses on the freedom of abandoning a car, rather than going through the usual process of trade-ins or of getting an evaluation from the wrecker.

In this section, we have introduced our idea, and then expanded on it. We can either continue to support this idea with more detail, or proceed to 'cap it off' by some means.

3 However, the poem is more meaningful when considered as an allegory for general freedom in life, rather than an apparently whimsical example. *Or:*

Beyond this trivial story lies a message about the importance of individualism and making up your own mind about things. *Or:*

Dawe uses this theme to stress the importance of valuing everyday items less casually, using our freedom of thought to find meaning even in small matters.

It may concern you that a summary seems to oversimplify. However, in the body of the essay you will get an opportunity to expand on, clarify and qualify your points; to discuss details in all their complexity.

A good summary will:

- *define* your understanding of the book or topic;
- *introduce* the major points; and even
- *interpret* it — that is, 'make something of it'.

Summary writing improves with practice, like most essay-writing skills.

EXERCISES

1 Choose whichever English text you have read or seen most recently. Write *no more* than three paragraphs summarising the main theme(s), main characters and situation. Use the 1–2–3 pattern.

2 Do this for every other English text you are studying. (Keep these exercises with your notes on that text, because they are useful study exercises.)

3 Summarise your understanding of a topic area in another subject such as Economics, Legal Studies or Geography. Some clues: What are the main points we need to know about that topic? What are the key terms, key facts, theories or issues?

Linking: 'signposted'

'Signposting' your argument makes a favourable impression, since it shows not only that you're organised but that you're courteously considering your reader as well. It's a common experience to settle into reading an essay and then find that one seems to have 'lost the plot' of what the writer is saying. Probably the writer has changed the topic but forgotten to tell the reader this. Signals need to be 'planted' into the next draft.

Using linking words and phrases helps to reinforce your essay by 'welding' the parts together. The actual words you need to use will be suggested by what you are saying. Here are some examples of connectives — ways of linking ideas:

Linking words

also	however
afterwards	subsequently
consequently	therefore
yet	meanwhile
moreover	thus

Linking phrases

as a result of this
some time later
a more significant factor
a fourth concern
for example

Linking between paragraphs

- Numbering: 'First we must consider the question of ... Secondly, we must look at ...'

- *Chronological*: (sequence of events) 'Some time after this first eruption of violence, policy changes began to be considered ...'

- *Contrast*: 'an even more important factor is ...'

  'The opposite viewpoint is discussed by Adam Smith, who claims that ...'

- *Cause/effect*: 'Because of this, the following changes were soon implemented ...'

- *Adding*: 'Another example of this phenomenon is ...'

- *Comparing*: 'A similar event was the case of Hutchinson Bros, a firm which ...'

- *Summarising*: 'Therefore, there is little narrative interest in this novel. However, the opposite is the case in *Looking for Alibrandi* ...'

EXERCISES

E

1 Look at any page of writing in a textbook and find as many linking words and phrases as you can.

2 Use linking words or phrases to join these sentences into one sentence.

   (a) There is nothing illegal about this.

      I am not perfectly happy about it.

   (b) I was walking down the street.

      I saw Natasha.

   (c) What are you going to do?

      Your casual job has finished.

   (d) My money is all gone.

      I will learn how to save in future.

(e) Your theory is debatable.

One could argue for or against it.

Quoting: specific

Your essay gives an opportunity to show what you know about the topic, and getting specific and detailed is a means of doing so. There are two quoting skills worth focusing on here:

- Quoting details
- Direct quotes.

Quoting details

A well-organised essay takes us on a journey, from the broad *overview* of the introduction, breaking it down to general *topics*, and then in the body of the essay, getting down to specific *detail*.

Say you wanted to write an essay about Louis Nowra's play *Cosi*, focusing on 'perspective'. This play is about a young man fresh out of university, directing his first play in an institution for the mentally ill, in 1971. At the *overview* level, you could say that some key themes are the following: conflicting perspectives, madness and sanity, art and reality. At the *topic* level, we look at various kinds of perspective, various forms of madness and sanity, and various representations of art and reality. At the *detail* level we discuss each topic in relation to particular people, scenes, themes and incidents (and so on).

The diagram on page 49 illustrates these three levels, concentrating on the 'Perspective' strand only.

In this diagram, you can see that we start with an overview of the themes of the work as a whole and then analyse the various strands of each theme, such as 'perspective', before getting even more detailed.

Many students restrict most of their discussion to the first two levels, which has two bad effects: you seem either not to be interested in the work very much, or not to know much more than the general picture. To quote details is far more impressive than running out of things to say, and just repeating vague generalities such as:

'Perspective is how you look at things' or 'different people have different perspectives' and so on.

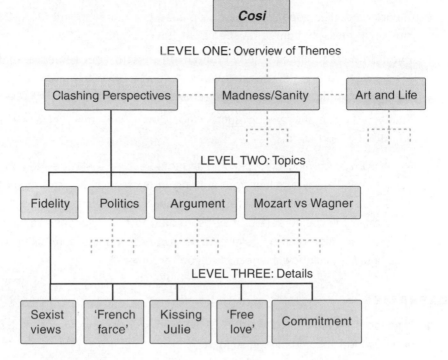

Next time you get stuck, start discussing more details: quote scenes or lines, incidents or uses of language that back up your statements and help you to develop your argument further.

Direct quoting

Quoting from books, from film dialogue or from speech is not one of the more difficult skills, but it is unimpressive when attention hasn't been paid to the rules:

- If quoting speech, put the actual speech (only) within inverted commas. Eric said: 'Please come immediately. My car won't start'.

- You can quote relevant authors by introducing them with phrases like: 'According to Jean Quirk …', or 'It is the opinion of James Brown that …'

- Do not change the actual wording *at all*. And check that you've written it 'word for word': it is very bad to misquote a professional writer, especially in English. In exams, you are not expected to remember quotes word for word. It is better to qualify your quotes. For example, write the following: Melvyn Bragg says words to the effect that ' … '

- You *can* leave words out, where this part of the quote is irrelevant to your argument, and it is preferable to do so. Use an *ellipsis* (set of three dots).

Tamara said 'For goodness' sake … please get more organised'. (Make your own guesses about what she might have said in-between!)

- If you do have to change the wording to fit in with your sentence, make this clear by putting the changed words in square brackets … Tamara said that '[we] couldn't organise a paper chase in a newsagency!'

- Finally, you can put a long quote (more than 2–3 lines) in a special indented block, like this:

> A word of warning: don't become a 'quote specialist' who tries to cobble an entire essay together from a string of quotes without an argument. These are sometimes referred to as 'straw essays'. Quotes alone will not 'prove' your point: details must be related to an argument; arguments must be supported by details. Once you have quoted something, you should explain how this relates to your argument.

EXERCISES

1 Describe a recent holiday you had. First, give an overview, then list topics, then describe actual details in support.

2 You are writing an essay about alcoholism, and have just quoted the following sentence from a reference book: 'Alcoholism is not merely a disease, but a major social problem'. Continue the discussion for a paragraph or two, explaining how this supports your argument about how alcoholism should be treated. (Make up details if necessary for this exercise.)

Explaining

Not only should you reveal details and facts, but you should also make sense of them. Don't rely on facts, figures and quotes to tell the story for you: *interpret* them for the reader.

For example, in Louis Nowra's play *Cosi* the social worker Justin says of the mental institution inmates: 'They're just normal people.' but then contradicts himself, saying: 'They are normal people who have done extraordinary things, thought extraordinary thoughts'.

But so what? We can develop the point further:

> The social worker, who is in a professional care role, shows confusion about the division between 'normal' and mad. If even the professionals have a confused perspective on the differences between sanity and

madness, what hope does the outsider Lewis have of perceiving the difference and communicating with the inmates effectively?

One detail has now been developed to make a more significant statement. Statistics usually need further discussion to explain their true significance: it is not enough to quote the current Balance of Payments figures, or the latest unemployment numbers; we need to know whether they are better or worse than expected, what effects they may have on other aspects of the economy, and so on.

Advanced skills 1: *analysis*

One difference between an average essay and a very good one can be that the better responses demonstrate a *critical* understanding of the issue. In other words, you don't take ideas for granted, but probe them further. Careful analysis of the following examples reveals that there are problems with the logic.

1 'Software piracy has always existed, so it always will.' This is a lazy argument that has no logical proof or reasoning. This kind of piracy was not a problem in Ancient Greece either!

2 'Any true Australian will believe in the flag we now fly as the one true flag.' There are a couple of problems with this idea: first of all, what is a 'true Australian'? Are Aboriginals, Torres Strait Islanders and migrants 'true Australians' or not?' The speaker doesn't clarify the point, but seems to be making a vague, emotional appeal.

3 'Arnold is an idiot, so anything he says can't be relied upon.' Arnold is truly in a bad way if this statement is literally true! Arguments should be based on logic, not personal attack.

4 'World weather patterns are definitely changing. I've never seen a November like this.' World weather patterns *might* be changing, but the speaker certainly can't deduce this from his or her limited life experience, nor speak of the 'world' from one part of the globe only.

5 'World War I was inevitable. Therefore so were all of the following events.' There are two assertions which are challengeable here: first, that the war was inevitable, and secondly, that its outbreak directly caused all succeeding events.

6 'I don't know what you're talking about; it's a load of rubbish.' Just because they don't understand it, doesn't mean it's wrong!

7 'Business is designed to meet public needs, so what's good for business is good for everybody.' Not necessarily, and not always! There is no real logical connection here.

8 'Because computers were designed by scientists, they have always been handy tools for scientists.' Many other things designed by scientists aren't of much use to them!

Learn to check the logic of your statements carefully, to test them out for yourself. Do they really 'hold water' or not?

Advanced skills 2: *fluency*

In English, you are marked (in part) on your ability to express yourself fluently and clearly in writing. This comes with practice of course, with wider reading and greater familiarity with language. But you should learn to look at your early drafts critically, and find ways to improve them. This example is from the introduction of a student's first draft social study essay.

> To answer most accurately what a total institution is, I *have quoted* Erving Goffman. I *have then* outlined the four *aspects believed essential to encompass being titled a* total institution, (she then lists these four points) ... (Italics are mine)

While the wording is still awkward at this stage, the general point can be understood: the writer is using Goffman's definition of a 'total institution', and will use four aspects of this definition. However, it is rather odd to say 'I have quoted' at the beginning of an essay, especially when she hasn't quoted him yet. To *quote* means to reproduce that writer's words exactly. What she means is that she is *referring* to Goffman's approach.

It is not usual to use the past tense in this way, as she does with 'I have quoted' and 'I have then outlined', especially at the start of an essay. We might use it later on, or in the conclusion: 'As I have shown ...' Generally one writes an English essay in the present tense. (See the sample essay in Chapter 6.) At times you can use the future tense here, as I have done with the underlined words of the revised passage below.

'Aspects believed essential to encompass being titled' is a rather hefty barrage of words, but what does it mean? For a start, *who* 'believes' this, and what does she mean by 'encompass being titled'? Impressive as the word 'encompass' is, it's not used quite accurately here. When in doubt it's easier to use plain words. Here's how a better version might look:

> To explain what a total institution is, reference *will be made* to Erving Goffman, and in particular to his description of the four characteristics of a total institution: …

Let's consider some of the changes made:

- Replacing 'answer' with 'explain'. The first word is not completely 'wrong', but the second belongs to the formal *register* (level) of essay English and is more suitable.
- Leaving out 'most accurately'—this phrase is not particularly helpful. On whose authority is this 'most accurate'? ('When in doubt, leave it out'.)
- Simplifying 'aspects believed essential to encompass being titled'. This pile-up of words gives the impression of uncertainty, hidden behind a wall of vague verbiage.
- Using a colon at the end of this sentence instead of a comma. Why? A colon is often used to introduce a list or some major point. Commas are used to separate words in a list, or different parts of the sentence from each other.

We can learn a number of things from this one example: that using fewer words can actually say 'more'. Get straight to the point, don't hide behind vague phrases and long strings of words, and don't use 'fancy words' unless you are sure of their meaning. (Once I explained the meaning of the word 'vocation'—a 'calling'—and asked a student to use it in a sentence. He came up with: 'My mother vocationed me in to dinner'. No, that's not quite right!)

These are key skills for improving your expression: clarifying your meaning, correcting grammar, word choice and punctuation. Linda Flower, in her book *Problem Solving Strategies for Writing*, comments that early drafts tend to be 'writer based'—they help the writer to get their ideas out, and tend to be structured according to the order in which thoughts came to the writer. That is a good start, but the good essay needs to transform that writer-based first draft into a reader-based, 'user friendly' essay with improved expression and structure.

A training run: *the five-paragraph essay*

In this chapter, we have looked at some of the *microskills* that contribute to a good essay. Now it's time to practise writing on the *macro* scale, putting it all together.

The five-paragraph essay is a very simple (but limited!) short essay form which gives good practice with the basics of essay structure. Simple as it is, few people 'get it right' first off. They have difficulty conforming to the rigid rules, and can't resist the urge to break them in some way!

Think of this form as a kind of game, or as a special challenge. The rules are simple: the five-paragraph essay allows you to advance an argument in the first paragraph, discuss three points to support it (one paragraph each), and cap it off in the final paragraph.

How to write a five-paragraph essay in eight steps

1 Choose any topic with which you are very familiar: any subject, topic or English text you have already studied. Ask yourself a question about it, e.g., 'What is the writer trying to say ...' or 'What do we know about the ancient Etruscans?'.

2 On a blank sheet of paper, write a brief answer in no more than a sentence. For example, 'The Australian poet Bruce Dawe is criticising the inanity of some aspects of modern life.'

3 Underneath this, list three points that support your argument.

Dawe criticises:

- the mass media
- consumerism
- lack of depth in conversation.

4 Draft your *first paragraph*. This paragraph must:

(a) state your argument;

(b) list the three points that support it.

(*Do not fail to do this!* This makes you plan ahead, from the very start.) If you have a clear idea of how to cap this argument off, then you could also refer to the final conclusion in some way, e.g. 'It will be seen that ... '

5 *Second paragraph*: Discuss your main, first point in full, giving details and relating it to your argument.

6 *Third paragraph:* Do the same, for the second point.

7 *Fourth paragraph:* Same as for the third point.

8 *Conclusion:* Summarise the previous discussion and try to cap it off somehow.

If you stick closely to the rules of the five-paragraph essay, you will see that it isn't really a hard trick; you'll soon decide it's rather boring and limiting. That also means that the essay form is actually really easy! But make sure you do produce at least one such essay, conforming completely to the rules. Use the method described above as your checklist and ask a friend to check it for you.

Congratulations! You've mastered the basic essay structure!

EXERCISES

(a) Read the following sample essay and underline all topic sentences.

(b) Underline the sentence that states the essay's main argument.

(c) Find as many 'linking' words as you can.

(d) What other 'microskills' does this essay use?

(e) Check this essay against the five-paragraph essay method described above. Does it meet all the requirements?

SAMPLE FIVE-PARAGRAPH ESSAY: LEARNING TO WRITE

One of the most confounding problems for the novice essay writer is the notion that writing is a talent that you either 'have' or don't have. The reality is quite different, however: this 'talent' is acquired by practice, by the development of separate 'microskills', and by getting guidance and feedback from a sensitive reader. It will be shown that work in these three areas will produce real progress, in time.

Many people who come back to study after years of absence complain that their mind has gone 'rusty', or that they find it hard to 'get into gear'. This suggests that writing and study are like physical activity: practising frequent, short periods of writing at regular intervals develops your mental 'fitness' better than a weekly study 'workout' after which you forget everything for another week. The essay writer needs regular practice, specifically with essays, and one more ingredient: a little time … No one gets 'fit' overnight.

The '*macroskill*' of writing is actually a combination of many different '*microskills*'— smaller skills needed in the writing process. Some of the more important of these are: sustaining an argument, organising data, expressing ideas clearly and concisely, and 'signposting'. Learning to write can be approached by working on these skills separately, or in various combinations, before they are all brought together in the essay itself.

If writing is, as the saying goes, 'a lonely business', the process of learning how to write doesn't really need to be. In fact, it is preferable to find someone to act as your 'mentor' or guide, reading your early drafts and helping you to improve them. Your mentor can be a parent, older brother or sister, family friend, or anyone who understands writing. However, good mentors can be hard to find: make sure that yours is not only knowledgeable, but that s/he gives you *positive* feedback and reassurance, and can show you how to improve on weaknesses. If you can afford it, a professional tutor is often the best help you will get in 'unlocking' your potential.

It has been demonstrated that the 'talent' of essay writing is, in fact, a skill, and that it can be learnt. Some key inputs to your learning process should be regular practice, the development of specific skills, and expert guidance. Once this skill is developed, your new-found 'talent' can be your key to the universe, for writing skills can help you get into your desired university or TAFE course and, beyond that, into the job of your dreams. In fact, if you continue to keep your mind 'fit', you'll use these skills throughout your career!

Chapter 5

Preparing for essays

In all subjects, as I said before, your essay can only be as good as the amount of study you've put into it. So before we look at putting the various skills together in the following chapter, it's important to discuss studying for essays.

And by the way, now that you are aware of 'linking', you should recognise that I am 'welding' this chapter with the previous and the following chapters, by referring to the link between the skills discussed in Chapter 4, and how they will be used in Chapter 6.

Studying for essays involves:

- Time organisation
- Focused study
- Note-taking
- Reading strategies.

It is possible to write an essay without having much to say. 'Waffle' tends to be full of vague terms, generalisations and half-thought-out ideas ... 'you know?' The writer might imagine that it 'looks alright' but in fact such essays are quickly spotted by experienced readers. One of the big shocks of the HSC years for many students is that the last-minute, studyless, just-dreamt-up-the-night-before essay doesn't do so well anymore. You will find this even more so at university or TAFE.

If you haven't researched, read widely, taken notes and thought carefully about your topic, you're not ready to write a good essay. You should, if possible, work out a rough essay plan before even starting to research an essay, to help you focus on the kind of information you need.

Let's look at these four key study skills:

Time organisation

To write a good essay takes time, so make time to give yourself the best chance.

- Start straightaway. Yes: the very day you're given the essay question, look at it carefully and ask yourself a few questions:
- What information would be required to answer the question?
- Do I know enough about the topic?
- What extra information do I need?
- What thoughts do I have about it at this stage?

I have said that the essay is like a par 3/4 golf hole, because it takes several shots to 'get there'. Also like golf, you get nowhere at all until you have at least teed off! Even if the first shot is woefully misdirected or dribbles to a miserable halt, you have made some progress. When you next strike, you should have a better sense of where you're headed, more determination, and, hopefully, a better aim once you've warmed up. With the essay, luckily, you don't lose points with each extra stroke you make: in fact, the more work you put into it, the better your essay usually is, up to a certain point.

- 'Incubate'. Let the ideas develop in your mind. Once you have come to a point where you simply can't think further about it, stop. It's surprising what ideas can 'hatch' out days later, even when you're not consciously thinking about the topic. But until you do the initial thinking, you won't 'hatch' anything. Planning in advance offers this advantage of making best use of your time, even when you're not studying! You can literally 'sleep on it'.

Focused study

Some students develop very inefficient study habits. The two extremes are: to read one book and take massive notes, virtually rewriting the book word for word, or, on the other hand, to write virtually nothing, trusting in memory completely. The first method of course will give you a pile of unwieldy 'junk', the second gives you very little at all. As we see below, it is better to consult several books or other sources in less detail than to read only one, cover to cover, including information that has no bearing on your study.

Focused study for essays means that you know what you are looking for, what is needed and what is not. Before starting your reading and research, make a list of all information you need, under separate headings. Under each heading write brief notes about what you know. Leave plenty of space under each one to add extra information, or use a separate sheet of paper for each. Also make a list of your specific questions: what 'proofs' are you looking for? What facts, figures or issues call for more information?

When rereading an English text it is usually helpful to take notes as you go, under thematic headings such as 'Characters', 'Plot', 'Themes', etc. Likewise you can take notes as you watch the video of a movie, 'pausing' occasionally, or download relevant Internet material directly into organised computer files. (Always remember to note the source and paste the URL into your file for reference.)

Note-taking

There are very many different ways of note-taking, none of them the sole correct form. Your notes are for you only; the most important thing is that they be easily identifiable, organised, clear, readable, and sufficiently complete so that, when you come back to read them some months later, they are still understandable. Whether you use a system of folders, cards, computer files or whatever, find an organised system that works well for you.

It is very helpful to make your system flexible so that your notes can be rearranged easily for essay-writing purposes. All your notes on characters, for example, might be on single loose leaves. Single sheets can be more helpful than lumping everything together in an exercise book. Use plenty of headings and subheadings (so that you can quickly find the right information). For computer notes, save them in appropriate directories and subdirectories to make files easy to locate.

Common student errors are:

- Taking notes randomly (whatever feels right)
- Writing down large chunks of information for no defined purpose
- Writing out whole pages word for word from the book (are you learning anything?).

Tip:

Work out your own 'shorthand' notation: it is handy to use symbols and abbreviations for commonly used words:

Use the first letter of a key term, capitalised, with a full stop after it: in English you might use L. for 'language'.

Other suggestions:
∴ therefore
+ also, in addition
→ (this led to …)
< Less than, smaller, or came before
> Greater than, after, more important.

Use standard symbols from different subjects, e.g., in Economics, 'Y' means 'income'.

Make up your own 'shorthand' for often-repeated words, as the need arises. Some symbols or abbreviations could be used for all subjects, whereas others might relate to one subject only. If there's a danger of forgetting what it stands for when you reread later, write a 'key' to these abbreviations somewhere on the first page of your notes.

(Computer users can use 'macros' to write commonly used words, or 'Search/Replace' options. By using the code 'e =', and later searching and replacing this 'string', I need type the word 'essay' once only for this entire book!)

Reading strategies

Reading becomes increasingly important in the HSC years, and is even more so with university and TAFE studies. Since you won't have time to read all textbooks and other sources 'cover to cover', you need to become familiar with different ways of using them. There are different ways of reading, and you should learn to vary your methods according to your purpose and to the style of the writing itself. If a book is particularly detailed and you need only general information, don't read it 'word for word'.

Reading is all about **anticipation**. Half-way through a sentence, we can often guess what's about to come next. (Do you ever finish sentences for people who are talking to you? It's a similar process.) Knowing the structure of writing also helps you read, anticipate and absorb more efficiently.

Books are usually structured 1–2–3 just like essays. They have an introduction, a body and a conclusion. You know that an introduction should give you the main argument, and introduce key topics. More detail on each point will be found in the body of the book. You can look for a final summing up, to see how the argument has progressed, or what final points are made, in the conclusion.

Selective reading

Wide reading is most helpful, but you certainly don't have to read every text available on a subject. Nor do you need to read every section, and every page of every book you consult. Different works have different strengths, so look at a range of them first before deciding which ones seem to offer you most. Concentrate on the Contents and Index, looking for your focus topics. Read the introduction quickly, and some of the first chapter, to get a general idea of the book. Sample a page at random to see if the writing is suited to your purposes. (Is it too technical, jargonistic; is the writer focused on themes that are unhelpful to you?)

Once you have chosen your reading sources, be selective in how you read them too, since not all sections may be helpful. A book is much easier to read the second time around, because you now have the 'big picture', and you know how sections relate to the whole work. So a preliminary skim or speed-read can make a full reading far more fruitful, as you'll absorb more information.

In your first reading, try not to use a dictionary very much. Often an unfamiliar word's meaning will become clear, especially if it's used often. You don't need to know the dictionary meaning of every word, so long as you can follow the discussion comfortably. Stopping too often slows you down and can lead to losing the thread of the argument. During a detailed reading, look up unfamiliar words, especially if they are used often. A good vocabulary is a great asset, now and for later study, and the best way to build one up is slowly, over time; so start now!

> **NOTE:** Here again, English is different to other essay-writing subjects because you do need to focus closely on the use of language. You should certainly read or view your prescribed texts fully and thoroughly, and at least twice. On your second, more detailed reading, look up unfamiliar words in a dictionary. You can practise selective reading when looking for supplementary material.

Skimming

Skimming is reading sections only, skipping to find the next section of interest. Concentrate on following the main ideas and blocking out detail. To read a chapter, it's a good idea to read the introductory paragraphs in full, then focus on topic sentences.

Scanning

In scanning you look only for a particular word or set of words, ignoring all else, and glancing over the pages rapidly. This has less value as a study skill, but it can help you find a particular passage quickly, or any references to one particular word or concept.

'Speed-reading'

It is possible to undertake short courses in this helpful skill. Don't get carried away by exaggerated claims, but it's certainly possible to build up a powerful Effective Reading Rate. (This term is a measure of how quickly one reads, compared to how much one absorbs and understands.) If you have time and money, and expect to do tertiary studies involving a lot of reading, this could be a good investment. Some selective colleges in the United States are said to require a minimum reading speed of 500 words per minute!

The key approach of speed-reading is not to read texts word for word but to 'open your eyes', your field of vision, and take in larger chunks of words at a time. It is a good start to practise concentrating on phrases, instead of single words.

Chapter 6

Essay writing 'by numbers'

Assuming that you have thoroughly researched your essay and organised your notes, you are ready to start the first draft. I jokingly call this chapter 'essay writing by numbers' but of course, writing is never so automatic as just 'joining the dots': it involves making choices in knowledge, argument, organisation and word usage. Unlike painting by numbers, the art of essay writing is genuinely creative.

The method described is only a suggested approach to help you get started, and the more familiar you become with essays the more you'll be able to find your own system. Be prepared to experiment, and see which ways work for you.

The method is summarised below and each point is then discussed in detail, just as the five-paragraph essay announces your points in advance, then expands on them. (However, in most essay writing, you can't use point form.)

Before studying this method, read the sample essay printed below. It is then reprinted with various explanations and notes. For those who are not familiar with the book, a short summary is given first. This is NOT part of the essay itself!

SUMMARY OF *THE STOLEN CHILDREN: THEIR STORIES*

The Stolen Children: Their Stories is a selection of texts related to *Bringing Them Home*, the Report of the National Inquiry into the separation of Indigenous children from their families 'by compulsion, undue pressure or duress'. These children were separated from their parents to be brought up as 'white' children, in foster homes or in institutions, and the report records the impact on these people's lives of the 'laws, practices and policies' of that time. *The Stolen Children* focuses on the testimonies of the 'storytellers' at that Inquiry, who tell of the terrible and lasting effects of separation on their health and happiness, their family relations, their identity and general adjustment to society. Most of them write from pain but without vindictiveness, and a number of them express forgiveness.

The focus of the book is a selection of personal testimonies from that report. Editor Carmel Bird also includes other texts to help put those testimonies in their social and historical contexts: a preface by the Inquiry chair Sir Ronald Wilson, the fifty-four recommendations of the Report and an afterword by historian Henry Reynolds.

An important section of the book is devoted to 'Perspectives' – a broad range of responses to the report from the Australian community, mostly from politicians, academics and other public figures. These range from qualified regret, through direct emotional sorrow, to veiled attacks on the report as being too subjective, unbalanced and emotional. Carmel Bird claims that 'to deny the past is to cast a dark shadow, to cripple the future' and appears to agree with Sir William Deane that many of the problems of Indigenous people now, stem from the past. She refers to the 'mounting theory that all Australians must learn to hear and to acknowledge'. Thus she hopes that *The Stolen Children* will help all Australians become more aware of the shameful legacy of the past as a means of creating a better future for Indigenous Australians.

Sample essay: *The stolen children*

The following sample essay is not perfect, and there are many other ways in which the question could have been answered. You may well disagree with the thesis and with particular points made. However, this sample illustrates the structure of an essay and some of the techniques involved. If need be, look up terms that are unclear to you.

How have the texts you have studied this year effectively shaped your understanding of the meaning of 'change'? In your answer you should refer to your prescribed text, ONE text from the prescribed stimulus booklet Changing, *and a variety of other related texts of your own choosing.*

(2001 HSC Specimen Paper, English [Standard and Advanced], Board of Studies NSW)

1 In this essay I will discuss how study of the prescribed text *The Stolen Children*, edited by Carmel Bird, and a range of other texts, has shaped my understanding of change in relation to the past and present lives of the Indigenous people of Australia. This understanding is formed from a series of perspectives, from historical to personal, to contemporary political and social perspectives. The most moving of these are the stories of Aboriginal children forcibly removed from their families. These Indigenous voices seek to be heard with real understanding, with empathy not sympathy. Bird believes that progress towards full Reconciliation can be achieved by our listening to these voices for if we 'can begin to imagine what life has been like for many Indigenous Australians over the past two hundred years' we will be led both to understand, and to act.

2 To understand the context of the Stolen Generation it is helpful to consider the historical background. Geoff Parr's collage 'The National Picture' (1985) not only reminds us of the radical change wrought by European settlement, but also suggests that we are still attempting to subdue rather than to understand Indigenous culture in a two-way sharing of perspectives. Henry Reynold's Afterword in *The Stolen Children* supports this, drawing comparisons between child stealing of the colonial period (pre-Federation) and that of the twentieth century and suggesting that most of the 'mistakes and cruelties' of the colonial time were repeated, and that Indigenous people have suffered almost as much from 'misguided benevolence as from the actions of those with evil intent.'

3 Duterreau's painting 'The Conciliation' (1840) is a reference point for Parr's work. A nattily dressed white man dominates this peacemaking meeting between himself and a large group of natives. The white man stands out powerfully in the foreground in contrast to the dark skin tones of the natives and the darkly forested hills. Almost prophet-like, with forefinger sternly raised, he appears to have subdued the dark masses singlehandedly, sealing the 'peace' with a handshake. The natives appear vulnerable and timid, although they seem to have the weapons and the numbers to overpower him if they so choose.

4 The painting's very title, perhaps unintentionally, reinforces the patronising effect. According to *The Macquarie Dictionary*, to 'conciliate' means 'to overcome the distrust or hostility of, by soothing or placating means; placate; win over. *Or* 2: To render compatible; reconcile.' This suggests that from the very early days when the British invaded and

settled in Australia, their approach to the original inhabitants of this land was to subdue them and forestall hostile behaviour, rather than trying to genuinely understand them or consider 'dual sovereignty' — a concept some colonists did once entertain, according to an article 'Who's sorry now?, by Debra Jopson (*The Sydney Morning Herald* 30 December, 2000).

5 Geoff Parr's collage parodies Duterreau's painting, as if to suggest that European Australia still has a 'colonial' attitude, and invites us to measure the change since 1840. He uses a similar cluster of people, except that the situation is reversed. Nearly all the people in the foreground would pass for 'white' or non-Indigenous people, and it is they who surround the one solitary Indigenous person. These Australians of an urban 'tribe' wield, instead of spears, surveying instruments, the 'weapons' with which European Australia took over and divided up the land. The land itself is now totally bare of trees and the only kangaroo in this picture has been skinned, symbolising the rape of nature. One person wields a portable radio whose antenna is also spear-like, symbolising the mass intrusion of European culture onto the land. Thus, Parr reminds us of the wholesale transformation of this continent by Europeans.

6 If colonial Australia appeased the natives, modern Australia is depicted as trying to bleach them out of the 'National Picture'. The sole Indigenous person is dressed in a neat white suit as if he or she had to put on a 'white skin' and business clothing to be accepted. His or her cultural identity is signalled by the Indigenous colours of red, black and yellow but in a very European style of dress, a scarf. In a sarcastic touch, Parr has superimposed the head of Truganini, the so-called 'last Tasmanian' over the head of this person, thus obliterating the figure's identity and reminding us of the attempted genocide in Tasmania, to which Carmel Bird also refers. 'Conciliation' has been replaced by erasure, whereas perhaps behind the white suit, that figure is like Penny's brother Trevor in *The Stolen Children*: 'Sometimes he gets suicidal .... He rings up and wants to kill himself .... People probably see on the surface that we've led successful lives. But that's on the surface.'

7 Another symbolic erasure of Indigenous perspectives is Parr's placement of a row of spear-carrying natives in the background. In Duterreau's painting the back row of natives stands as a part of, and in reinforcement to, the native group in the foreground. In Parr's collage they look like grey statues hidden behind the corrugated iron fence that forms a barrier between the modern group and the original inhabitants of the land. The

suggestion is that white Australia has tried to 'fence off' and contain our history of Indigenous relations. However, those grey ghosts have endured for over two centuries and appear unlikely to go away, suggesting that at some stage Australia will need to reconcile with the traditional owners.

8   Parr's parody suggests that modern Australian culture is still trying to nullify the Indigenous 'threat', attempting to erase both Australia's 'black history' of invasion and genocide, and Indigenous culture itself. His 1985 collage is supported by later texts such as the *Bringing Them Home* Report (1997), and various perspectives in *The Stolen Children* as well as in views from other Australians. A letter to the editor by Brendan Jones under the heading 'Racist, undemocratic: that was Federation' (*The Sydney Morning Herald*, 6 January 2001) claims that 'Australia's first law—the "Federal Immigration Act"— enshrined the White Australia Policy'. The stories told in *The Stolen Children* explain the terrible effects of this attempted cultural erasure on certain victims, but also offer a perspective on how true reconciliation can be furthered.

9   Paul's account begins by expressing the loss of identity he suffered at the mercy of governmental control as 'State Ward Number 54321'. This label blocks out his mother, his family, his name and his Aboriginality. The damage inflicted on these children was lasting. It is as if their lives have been taken hostage, and even today they cannot reveal their past under their real names. John adds: 'And we'll always be prisoners while our files are in archives'. If the victims did not lose their families altogether, many of them were permanently estranged from their families, their own mother, and in some cases, from their Indigenous identity. Eric yearns for strong family ties, yet finds family meetings painful. This pain is in addition to the common pattern of rejection and abuse from the 'white' family or institutions that were meant to 'assimilate' them. Many storytellers describe degradation, bullying and abuse from the society in which they were forced to live.

10   Despite the devastating blows Paul has received, his anger is mostly contained to passing comments, and his final emphasis is on positive things: his survival, and treasuring the 'handful of precious memories' of his mother. Like the other storytellers, he expresses no desire for revenge or compensation, his words commanding only a fair hearing and understanding. In this respect he leads by example, frequently mirroring the 'whitefella's' perspective — quoting their reports, comments and attitudes frequently, thus pointing the way for us to listen to and

understand his own perspective. Reconciliation is not about the colonial mission of civilising and placating the natives but about a mutual, respectful sharing of perspectives.

11 Carol admits to having a 'big mouth' but then states only that 'I am going to make sure that the world knows what really happened to our people' because for her and other storytellers it is important that the truth be told and understood. Murray goes further, writing a piece specifically for this book where he directly addresses the 'dear reader and travelling companion', inviting us to share his sad life. These confidential submissions are generous gestures towards reconciliation, overcoming pain with dignity, honesty and lack of bitterness. They challenge us to respond with equal understanding and generosity, as many Australians have done in signing 'Sorry Books', Marching for Reconciliation and so on. However, responses from the Federal Government at that time had shortcomings.

12 The response of the Prime Minister is important as it symbolises the attitude of the Australian Government. While the excerpt of John Howard's parliamentary speech begins by attacking unnamed parties who apparently deny that Aboriginal and Torres Strait Islander (ATSI) people are 'profoundly disadvantaged', closer analysis of his language suggests that he is not listening to ATSI voices. Howard soon qualifies his concern by stating that 'We are not obsessed with symbolism. We are concerned, though, with practical outcomes.' Thus he trivialises calls for a formal apology as mere 'symbolism', and presumably not 'practical' enough. One is reminded of storyteller Penny's comment: 'Strange how the bureaucracy adopt the materialistic yardstick when measuring poverty/ deprivation/ neglect.' The same seems to apply to governmental views on reconciliation. John Howard implies that those who want an apology are 'obsessed', but the storytellers would say the wound won't heal until it has been treated. Perhaps it is not 'practical' to demand reconciliation solely on Howard's own restricted terms.

13 Rather than apologising, Howard expresses 'deep sorrow' for those who suffered, stipulating that this was the work of 'past generations', thus distancing the Government from blame and reducing the likelihood of an apology or compensation. He takes for granted that 'all members of the House can understand the pain and trauma', yet gives little sign that he has heeded the message of the storytellers and other Indigenous voices that the healing process requires recognition from Australia's foremost

'elder', by means of an apology. By setting his own terms, Howard reinforces the old message that 'white man knows best' and that Indigenous perspectives can be ignored.

14 Howard's attempts to portray his Government positively, lead him into misleading rhetoric. In ruling out compensation he is clearly not 'putting his money where his mouth is'. Howard's argument is a little misleading in stating that current generation(s) of Australians can not be held accountable or 'regarded as guilty for the acts of earlier generations' since many of the people involved in these hurtful practices are still alive. Carol, after detailing the shocking practices of some priests, observes that they are 'still alive, they're still working down South'. Many of the horrors detailed in the report happened in Howard's own lifetime. Nor do the report or the storytellers ask Australians to feel guilty or accountable, as Howard suggests. The report makes fifty-four recommendations of a 'practical' nature to help recognise and heal the hurt that has been done, including apologies and reparations by 'all Australian Parliaments'.

15 Howard implies that the stolen generation's story is 'history', thereby subtly relegating issues to the past, yet emphasises Australia's 'heroic achievement' over the past two hundred years, as if the gains of Australia as a whole outweigh the severe losses of a minority. He refers to our treatment of Indigenous people as a 'blemish'. A blemish is only 'skin deep', an unsightly but minor fault in the smooth complexion of 'white' Australia. As with Geoff Parr's white-suited Indigenous figure, official Australia seems more interested in shutting out the past, and in surface appearances, than the deeper reality.

16 Various texts produced since *The Stolen Children* support Parr's theme and confirm that the Federal Government still fails to heed the message. The article 'Who's sorry now?' by Debra Jopson discusses the 'faltering tracks' of official Reconciliation, damaged by the Prime Minister's controversial announcement that a final reconciliation document would not be achieved by the scheduled wind-up time of 31 December 2000, an act which the Aboriginal activist Charles Perkins (since deceased) had described as 'despicable'. Jopson's introduction details an eye disorder that the new Minister of Aboriginal Affairs has admitted to. She suggests that Phillip Ruddock's weakness is symbolic of the government's 'depth of vision problem in indigenous affairs' and quotes the Reconciliation Council's final report which states that lasting reconciliation 'is not a foregone conclusion'.

17 Together with this lack of depth in vision, Jopson detects no depth of commitment. She notes that 'An argument can still be made that reconciliation has been nothing but a cruel trick in which powerful figures made a pretence at change without ruffling the status quo'. She also quotes an indigenous artist, Bronwyn Bancroft, who has described it as '"*reconcealiation*", or covering up the true history and plight of Aborigines all over again' — a description that echoes the erasure of Indigenous culture and history in Geoff Parr's collage. (Italics mine.)

18 My understanding of the meaning of 'change' is shaped by different perspectives on the destructive effects of change wrought by European invasion and settlement on the traditional owners of this country. Indigenous Australians have survived horrendous, prolonged suffering with dignity and pride, even to pass on a message of forgiveness, and hope for positive change. Both 'symbolic' and practical Reconciliation remain important goals for all Australians. Boori ('Monty') Pryor may agree with Carmel Bird's view that all Australians should broaden their perspectives with 'imagination' and understanding, as he says that 'Reconciliation has to start within yourself'. It starts with 'day one, Invasion Day … We have to acknowledge the past so we can understand and accept it and then go on, move on from there into a better future'. Nothing less than true understanding and generosity can match the powerful words of the survivors of the Stolen Generation, and the way forward for all Australians is with open ears and an open heart.

Sample essay with annotations

The same essay is reproduced below, but with comments and explanations following each paragraph. I have even created 'headings', to signal the essay's structure!

- Paragraphs are numbered.

- The key parts of topic sentences are underlined.

- The argument statement is double underlined.

- Comments are in *italics*.

- Keywords from the question are in **bold type**.

- Keywords related to detailed discussion of aspects of the argument are in reverse type .

How have the texts you have studied this year effectively shaped your understanding of the meaning of 'change'? In your answer you should refer to your prescribed text, ONE text from the prescribed stimulus booklet Changing, *and a variety of other related texts of your own choosing.*

(2001 HSC Specimen Paper, English [Standard and Advanced], Board of Studies NSW)

INTRODUCTION

1   In this essay I will discuss how study of the prescribed text *The Stolen Children*, edited by Carmel Bird, and a range of other texts, has **shaped my understanding of change** in relation to the past and present lives of the Indigenous people of Australia. This understanding is formed from a series of perspectives , from historical to personal, to contemporary political and social perspectives. The most moving of these are the stories of Aboriginal children forcibly removed from their families. These Indigenous voices seek to be heard with real understanding , with empathy not sympathy. Bird believes that progress towards full Reconciliation can be achieved by our listening to these voices, for if we 'can begin to imagine what life has been like for many Indigenous Australians over the past two hundred years' we will be led both to understand, and to act.

This first paragraph accomplishes three important things: first 'echoing' the question to put me on track (in the topic sentence), secondly introducing some aspects I will treat (reverse type), and then stating my own argument (double-underlined). The aspect of 'perspective' comes from the 2001 Focus Area: 'Changing Perspective' which the prescribed text is related to.

SECTION NO. 1: HISTORICAL PERSPECTIVE

2   To understand the context of the Stolen Generation it is helpful to consider the historical background. Geoff Parr's collage 'The National Picture' (1985) not only reminds us of the radical **change** wrought by European settlement, but also suggests that we are still attempting to subdue rather than to understand Indigenous culture in a two-way sharing of perspectives . Henry Reynold's Afterword in *The Stolen Children* supports this, drawing comparisons between child stealing of the colonial period (pre-Federation) and that of the twentieth century and suggesting that most of the 'mistakes and cruelties' of the colonial time were

repeated, and that Indigenous people have suffered almost as much from 'misguided benevolence as from the actions of those with evil intent.'

I have chosen to start with the visual 'text' from the 2001 Stimulus Booklet first, rather than the main, prescribed text, on the organisational principle of chronology: sketching the historical context before examining present day conditions, since the history helps explain the present. Discussion of this topic begins with reference to the essay question's focus on 'change'. The context of any text is very important to understanding its meaning. Referring to ONE text from the stimulus booklet is a requirement of the question.

3 <u>Duterreau's painting 'The Conciliation' (1840) is a reference point for Parr's work</u>. A nattily dressed white man dominates this peacemaking meeting between himself and a large group of natives. The white man stands out powerfully in the foreground in contrast to the dark skin tones of the natives and the darkly forested hills. Almost prophet-like, with forefinger sternly raised, he appears to have subdued the dark masses singlehandedly, sealing the 'peace' with a handshake. The natives appear vulnerable and timid, although they seem to have the weapons and the numbers to overpower him if they so choose.

Understanding Parr's work in context entails discussing a preceding work first.

4 <u>The painting's very title, perhaps unintentionally, reinforces the patronising effect</u>. According to *The Macquarie Dictionary*, to 'conciliate' means 'to overcome the distrust or hostility of, by soothing or placating means; placate; win over. *Or* 2: To render compatible; reconcile.' This suggests that from the very early days when the British invaded and settled in Australia, their approach to the original inhabitants of this land was to subdue them and forestall hostile behaviour, rather than trying to genuinely understand them or consider 'dual sovereignty' — a concept some colonists did once entertain, according to an article 'Who's sorry now?', by Debra Jopson (*The Sydney Morning Herald* 30 December, 2000).

It is always a good idea to provide definitions of key terms, particularly if they are rather abstract or simply not clear to you. The above paragraph (like some later discussion) pays close attention to language, which is generally helpful in English.

5 Geoff Parr's collage parodies Duterreau's painting, as if to suggest that European Australia still has a 'colonial' attitude, and invites us to measure the change since 1840. He uses a similar cluster of people, except that the situation is reversed. Nearly all the people in the foreground would pass for 'white' or non-Indigenous people, and it is they who surround the one solitary Indigenous person. These Australians of an urban 'tribe' wield instead of spears, surveying instruments, the 'weapons' with which European Australia took over and divided up the land. The land itself is now totally bare of trees and the only kangaroo in this picture has been skinned, symbolising the rape of nature. One person wields a portable radio whose antenna is also spear-like, symbolising the mass intrusion of European culture onto the land. Thus, Parr reminds us of the wholesale transformation of this continent by Europeans.

This paragraph relates the discussion back to the essay question, which is focused on our understanding of 'change'. The final sentence 'caps off' the discussion with a mini-summary of Parr's work.

6 If colonial Australia appeased the natives, modern Australia is depicted as trying to bleach them out of the 'National Picture'. The sole Indigenous person is dressed in a neat white suit as if he or she had to put on a 'white skin' and business clothing to be accepted. His or her cultural identity is signalled by the Indigenous colours of red, black and yellow but in a very European style of dress, a scarf. In a sarcastic touch, Parr has superimposed the head of Truganini, the so-called 'last Tasmanian' over the head of this person, thus obliterating the figure's identity and reminding us of the attempted genocide in Tasmania, to which Carmel Bird also refers. 'Conciliation' has been replaced by erasure, whereas perhaps behind the white suit, that figure is like Penny's brother Trevor in *The Stolen Children*: 'Sometimes he gets suicidal …. He rings up and wants to kill himself …. People probably see on the surface that we've led successful lives. But that's on the surface.'

While the first paragraph devoted to Parr's work gives a broad description, relating it to the earlier painting, this second paragraph develops a more specific point: the attempted erasure of Indigenous identity and culture, thus introducing the aspects of 'identity' and 'erasure'.

7 Another symbolic erasure of Indigenous perspectives is Parr's placement of a row of spear-carrying natives in the background. In Duterreau's painting the back row of natives stands as a part of, and in

reinforcement to, the native group in the foreground. In Parr's collage they look like grey statues hidden behind the corrugated iron fence that forms a barrier between the modern group and the original inhabitants of the land. The suggestion is that white Australia has tried to 'fence off' and contain our history of Indigenous relations. However, those grey ghosts have endured for over two centuries and appear unlikely to go away, suggesting that at some stage Australia will need to reconcile with the traditional owners.

This paragraph further supports the theme with another example, finally relating it back to the argument about reconciliation. Note the detailed discussion of the 'visual language' of these texts.

8 Parr's parody suggests that <u>modern Australian culture is still trying to nullify the Indigenous 'threat', attempting to erase both Australia's 'black history' of invasion and genocide, and Indigenous culture itself</u>. His 1985 collage is supported by later texts such as the *Bringing Them Home* Report (1997), and various perspectives in *The Stolen Children* as well as in views from other Australians. A letter to the editor by Brendan Jones under the heading 'Racist, undemocratic: that was Federation' (*The Sydney Morning Herald*, 6 January 2001) claims that 'Australia's first law—the "Federal Immigration Act"— enshrined the White Australia Policy'. The stories told in *The Stolen Children* explain the terrible effects of this attempted cultural erasure on certain victims, but also offer a perspective on how true reconciliation can be furthered.

This paragraph completes discussion of the historical background with a mini-summary, reverts to the theme of 'true reconciliation' which is a central part of the argument, and links to the next point of discussion: stories told in the prescribed text (another requirement of the question). Also note that the essay demonstrates a wide range of reading and research. This is obviously very helpful, particularly for English Advanced students.

Section No. 2: Stories of the stolen children

9 Paul's account begins by expressing the loss of identity he suffered at the mercy of governmental control as 'State Ward Number 54321'. This label blocks out his mother, his family, his name and his Aboriginality. <u>The damage inflicted on these children was lasting</u>. It is as if their lives have been taken hostage, and even today they cannot reveal their past

under their real names. John adds: 'And we'll always be prisoners while our files are in archives'. If the victims did not lose their families altogether, many of them were permanently estranged from their families, their own mother, and in some cases, from their Indigenous identity. Eric yearns for strong family ties, yet finds family meetings painful. This pain is in addition to the common pattern of rejection and abuse from the 'white' family or institutions that were meant to 'assimilate' them. Many storytellers describe degradation, bullying and abuse from the society in which they were forced to live.

Discussion in this next section is still focused on the central theme of 'identity'. Note that the body of the argument, throughout this essay, is divided into sections according to chronological order: from the older texts, to the government report, responses to the report, and then more recent texts. A different essay might organise the points in a very different way, such as treating different themes in order of importance. The organisational principle I have used is a way of handling the question's emphasis on a variety of texts, but also offers the bonus of helping us to map changing practices over time.

10 Despite the devastating blows Paul has received, his anger is mostly contained to passing comments, and his final emphasis is on positive things: his survival, and treasuring the 'handful of precious memories' of his mother. Like the other storytellers, he expresses no desire for revenge or compensation, his words commanding only a fair hearing and understanding . In this respect he leads by example, frequently mirroring the 'whitefellas's' perspective — quoting their reports, comments and attitudes frequently, thus pointing the way for us to listen to and understand his own perspective . Reconciliation is not about the colonial mission of civilising and placating the natives but about a mutual, respectful sharing of perspectives.

Again, the discussion is linked back to the essay's argument, about understanding and reconciliation.

11 Carol admits to having a 'big mouth' but then states only that 'I am going to make sure that the world knows what really happened to our people' because for her and other storytellers it is important that the truth be told and understood. Murray goes further, writing a piece specifically for this book where he directly addresses the 'dear reader and travelling companion', inviting us to share his sad life. These confidential

submissions are generous gestures towards reconciliation , overcoming pain with dignity, honesty and lack of bitterness. They challenge us to respond with equal understanding and generosity, as many Australians have done in signing 'Sorry Books', Marching for Reconciliation and so on. However, responses from the Federal Government at that time had shortcomings.

The theme is capped off and then linked to the next discussion point in the last sentence.

SECTION NO. 3: RESPONSES TO THE *BRINGING THEM HOME* REPORT

12 The response of the Prime Minister is important as it symbolises the attitude of the Australian Government. While the excerpt of John Howard's parliamentary speech begins by attacking unnamed parties who apparently deny that Aboriginal and Torres Strait Islander (ATSI) people are 'profoundly disadvantaged', closer analysis of his language suggests that he is not listening to ATSI voices. Howard soon qualifies his concern by stating that 'We are not obsessed with symbolism . We are concerned, though, with practical outcomes.' Thus he trivialises calls for a formal apology as mere 'symbolism', and presumably not 'practical' enough. One is reminded of storyteller Penny's comment: 'Strange how the bureaucracy adopt the materialistic yardstick when measuring poverty/ deprivation/ neglect.' The same seems to apply to governmental views on reconciliation. John Howard implies that those who want an apology are 'obsessed', but the storytellers would say the wound won't heal until it has been treated. Perhaps it is not 'practical' to demand reconciliation solely on Howard's own restricted terms.

In this section, I discuss language quite closely, always in relation to the argument. Also the aspect of 'symbolism' is now foregrounded.

13 Rather than apologising, Howard expresses 'deep sorrow' for those who suffered, stipulating that this was the work of 'past generations', thus distancing the Government from blame and reducing the likelihood of an apology or compensation. He takes for granted that 'all members of the House can understand understand the pain and trauma', yet gives little sign that he has heeded the message of the storytellers and other Indigenous voices that the healing process requires recognition from Australia's foremost 'elder', by means of an apology. By setting his own

terms, <u>Howard reinforces the old message that 'white man knows best' and that Indigenous perspectives can be ignored</u>.

Based on wider reading, I am able to place Howard's speech in the wider political context of demands for an apology, something his excerpted speech doesn't mention.

14 <u>Howard's attempts to portray his Government positively, lead him into misleading rhetoric</u>. In ruling out compensation he is clearly not 'putting his money where his mouth is'. Howard's argument is a little misleading in stating that current generation(s) of Australians can not be held accountable or 'regarded as guilty for the acts of earlier generations' since many of the people involved in these hurtful practices are still alive. Carol, after detailing the shocking practices of some priests, observes that they are 'still alive, they're still working down South'. Many of the horrors detailed in the report happened in Howard's own lifetime. Nor do the report or the story tellers ask Australians to feel guilty or accountable, as Howard suggests. The report makes fifty-four recommendations of a 'practical' nature to help recognise and heal the hurt that has been done, including apologies and reparations by 'all Australian Parliaments'.

The discussion is detailed and analytical here. See 'Advanced skills' in the 'Microskills' chapter, especially for English Advanced students! 'Rhetoric' is the art of persuasion, and is a very handy 'language' term to know.

15 Howard implies that the stolen generation's story is 'history', thereby subtly relegating issues to the past, and emphasises Australia's 'heroic achievement' over the past two hundred years, as if the gains of Australia as a whole outweigh the severe losses of a minority. He refers to our treatment of Indigenous people as a 'blemish'. A blemish is only 'skin deep', an unsightly but minor fault in the smooth complexion of 'white' Australia. As with Geoff Parr's white-suited Indigenous figure, <u>official Australia seems more interested in shutting out the past, and in surface appearances, than the deeper reality</u>.

This section is rounded off by referring back to Parr's central themes.

SECTION NO. 4: LATER TEXTS

16 <u>Various texts since *The Stolen Children* support Parr's theme and confirm that the Federal Government still fails to heed the message</u>. The article 'Who's sorry now?' by Debra Jopson, discusses the 'faltering tracks' of official `Reconciliation`, damaged by the Prime Minister's controversial announcement that a final Reconciliation document would not be achieved by the scheduled wind-up time of 31 December 2000, an act which the Aboriginal activist Charles Perkins (since deceased) had described as 'despicable'. Jopson's introduction details an eye disorder that the new Minister of Aboriginal Affairs has admitted to. She suggests that Phillip Ruddock's weakness is `symbolic` of the government's 'depth of vision problem in indigenous affairs' and quotes the Reconciliation Council's final report which states that lasting reconciliation 'is not a foregone conclusion'.

Further use is made of wider reading to put the prescribed text in context, and in a different genre (newspaper feature article). Although use of the word 'symbolic' is only made in passing above, it serves to remind the reader that all consumers of texts are well aware of the importance of symbolism. This comments on Howard's suggestion that symbolism is not important.

17 <u>Together with this lack of depth in vision, Jopson detects no depth of `commitment`</u>. She notes that 'An argument can still be made that `reconciliation` has been nothing but a cruel trick in which powerful figures made a pretence at change without ruffling the status quo'. She also quotes an indigenous artist, Bronwyn Bancroft, who has described it as '"*reconcealiation*", or covering up the true history and plight of Aborigines all over again' — a description that echoes the erasure of Indigenous culture and history in Geoff Parr's collage. (Italics mine.)

I conclude the final section of discussion by relating it back to the question of reconciliation and Parr's theme, with which the body of the essay started. It also introduces the final, important aspect of 'commitment'. In this section I would have discussed Boori 'Monty' Pryor's book as another Indigenous text, but this has been omitted for space considerations.

CONCLUSION

18 <u>My **understanding** of the meaning of **'change'** is shaped by different perspectives</u> on the destructive effects of change wrought by European invasion and settlement on the traditional owners of this country.

Indigenous Australians have survived horrendous, prolonged suffering with dignity and pride, even to pass on a message of forgiveness, and hope for positive **change**. Both 'symbolic' and practical Reconciliation remain important goals for all Australians. Boori ('Monty') Pryor may agree with Carmel Bird's view that all Australians should broaden their perspectives with 'imagination' and understanding, as he says that 'Reconciliation has to start within yourself'. It starts with 'day one, Invasion Day … We have to acknowledge the past so we can understand and accept it and then go on, move on from there into a better future'. Nothing less than true understanding and generosity can match the powerful words of the survivors of the Stolen Generation, and the way forward for all Australians is with open ears and an open heart.

This conclusion first reverts to the original question, then summarises, without merely repeating, the main argument. It also starts to 'cap off' the discussion by taking a more personal angle. Also, the original argument statement (see first paragraph) has been added to with the reference to symbolic and practical reconciliation, and I have chosen to let my thesis be restated by an Indigenous voice rather than by myself. As mentioned above, Boori Pryor's book would have been treated in the previous section.

Outline of twelve steps in essay writing 'by numbers'

The following twelve steps form a suggested method to help you learn the process of essay writing, but you should be prepared to find whatever methods work best for you. The method has been devised with 'take-home', researched essays in mind. Exam essays are discussed in Chapter 9.

1 **Analyse the question.**
   Find the keywords: subject, topic, aspect.

2 **Note the 'doing' words.**

3 **Organise data.**
   (a) Research
   (b) Assemble
   (c) Group
   (d) Rank/order

4 **Develop an argument or theme.**

5 **Plan the essay.**
The keyhole essay plan.
Other ways of planning: 'mind maps'.
The long walk.
Audition.
The structured response.

6 **Draft an introduction.**
(a) 'Echo', re-state or paraphrase the question.
(b) State your argument.
(c) Indicate the key points.
(d) (Anticipate your conclusion).

7 **Check your introduction against the checklist.**

8 **Draft the body of the essay.**
Treat each topic in turn.
Sustain your argument.
Refer back to your argument.
Give specific 'proofs'.
Use 'transition' or linking words and phrases.
Paragraph carefully.
Qualify your statements.

9 **Draft the conclusion.**
Reread the essay question.
Reread the introduction.
Summarise your argument and main points.
Cap off your argument.

10 **Redraft the essay.**
Make a fresh start.
Keep an open mind.

11 **Macro-editing**
Subtraction
Addition

12 **Micro-editing**
Sentence length
Grammar
Spelling

Each of the previous steps is treated below, in detail. Note that this is only a suggested sequence, and it is common to do some of these steps 'out of order' or to go back to a particular step to change something.

Step 1: Analyse the question

Find the keywords: subject, topic, aspect

The importance of answering the question has been emphasised repeatedly. Your first step in doing so is to make sure you understand the question, by focusing on keywords. Let's look at the essay question again:

> *How have the texts you have studied this year effectively shaped your understanding of the meaning of 'change'? In your answer you should refer to your prescribed text, ONE text from the prescribed stimulus booklet* Changing, *and a variety of other related texts of your own choosing.*

Keywords

Subject keywords: (Topic Area—Change)

Topic keywords: texts, shaped, understanding of change

Aspect keywords: Not supplied. Therefore we have to determine what aspect of the topic we will treat. I used the term 'Changing perspective' from the specific focus area, and also supplied terms such as 'reconciliation' and 'understanding'.

Note: This question is quite 'open', and thus puts the onus on you to decide what aspect to treat. You should indicate these aspects very early in your essay, as I have done in Paragraph 1 of the sample essay.

The following would be a more 'closed' version of the question, as it supplies an aspect:

> *How have the texts you have studied this year effectively shaped your understanding of **the challenges posed by 'change'**? In your answer you should refer to your prescribed text, ONE text from the prescribed stimulus booklet* Changing, *and a variety of other related texts of your own choosing.*

In this version, the aspect keyword would be 'challenges'. Other keywords remain the same.

Step 2: Note the 'doing' words

In the majority of questions a clear requirement is specified, which we must meet. In this example, we are told to *refer to* the prescribed text, one from the stimulus booklet and 'a variety of other texts', so the question does place a lot of emphasis on the range of texts you must refer to.

The best understanding of what you're required to do will always be found in the *context* of the question, that is, in consideration of the question as a whole. However, the Board of Studies has standardised the use of instruction words, and some of the most common are reproduced at the end of Chapter 9.

Note: Not all questions will contain 'doing' words. For example: 'Why would this poem be a good inclusion in an anthology for young Australians?'

Step 3: Organise data

Steps 1 and 2 are concerned with understanding and 'listening to' the question. In Steps 3 and 4 we begin to prepare our detailed answer by rereading the texts, further researching, and then organising the data into manageable sets of notes.

(a) Research

Make a list of key topics before researching. For the sample essay, information needed to be researched for four broad topics, which could in turn be divided into smaller subtopics. The topics were:

- change

- changing perspectives

- identity

- reconciliation.

To write this essay, I first read or viewed all the main texts quickly, and then read or viewed them again, this time taking notes with special reference to the themes I had identified. After this, I looked for extra texts to give me more information and to check on some questions and facts I had jotted down, e.g. 'is that really a photograph of Truganini?'

(b) Assemble

Bring all your notes together, organised in plastic clip folders, manila folders or some other way, so you can find the information quickly. It may be worthwhile to create a master list of notes, citing where to find various bits of information. (Again, computers would be optimal here as you can copy and paste information to exactly where you want it.)

I had notes about each text I planned to use, as well as separate notes under the heading of different themes I was exploring.

(c) Group

In Chapter 3 we saw that there are different ways of grouping and ordering information. For a question about the themes of a particular work or collection of poems, you would group data under thematic headings. For a question based on the use of language, your headings would relate to various aspects of language.

While studying for *The Stolen Children* I took notes and listed ideas under the headings of 'change', 'changing perspective', 'identity' and 'reconciliation', as these themes all related to my argument. The following is a sample of my notes, not all of which were used directly in the essay. In places, I indicate which text has the relevant information. (As you will see below, I later chose to reorganise the notes differently.)

ESSAY NOTES
THE STOLEN CHILDREN: DIFFERENT PERSPECTIVES

Change

The world that the Indigenous people lived in for 60 thousand years or more has been totally changed, both environmentally and socially (use Parr's collage).

It is impossible for most of them to live in the way they used to and while not all change is bad, European invasion was a disaster for native people.

Fortunately 'white' attitudes to Indigenous people have changed a lot since colonial days and since Federation (still racist in 1901!).

Finally they did get a vote and legal recognition of land rights (news clippings, Henry Reynolds).

Major change is needed in the future to help fix the many problems that Indigenous people face.

(Recommendations of the Report)

Changing perspective

Australia at Federation had racist attitudes both to the traditional owners and to immigrants (news clippings and letters to the editor).

Attitudes to the Indigenous peoples have *changed* greatly over time.

The 'stolen children' practice may have seemed correct to many Australians at the time, but time gives another perspective to it.

Many people just assumed that 'white is better' but what evidence was there for this attitude?

We can learn a lot from Indigenous people and sharing perspectives also promotes understanding and better communication.

It takes a concerted effort to jolt ourselves out of old attitudes and habits.

Identity

Forced separation attacked both the personal/family identity as well as cultural identity (various storytellers).

Identity is essential to psychological wellbeing (Eric's psychiatrist).

Intervention at an early age created damage to identity that was apparently irreversible.

Howard suggests that 'symbolic' measures aren't important, and yet respects the Australian flag, ANZAC ceremonies, Olympic openings, etc.

Some of the adoptive families and foster institutions never accepted the kids as equals, so they had nowhere where self-esteem was possible.

Reconciliation

A genuine dialogue is two-way.

So we must be prepared to genuinely listen to very different points of view and different practices. E.g. to recognise native law is a challenge to orthodox law.

Many positive gestures towards reconciliation have been made (Sydney Olympics, sorry books, walks in each Australian capital city, etc.) and we need to keep building on this.

Reconciliation is one form of positive change which is needed along with 'practical' reconciliation.

(d) Rank/order

The final step in organising data is to decide on the sequence in which to discuss topics. Usually we start with the broad picture, the overview, then discuss points in detail, one after the other. There are two levels of ordering or ranking:

1 order of topics

2 ordering points *within* each topic.

Originally I had planned to discuss topics 'theme by theme'. However, once I had started trying to rank and order my notes, I soon realised that a better way to organise them was on the basis of 'text by text' in chronological (time) order. This was appropriate to deal with a variety of texts in an order that would show 'change' (a central theme) over time, from early Australia till very recently.

Therefore I started to order my notes around this *order of topics*: the four main chronological periods. Points within each topic were ordered in the following way.

1 *Historical perspective:* Most important text first—stimulus booklet texts, followed by comment from an historian. (Because booklet texts were central to the argument).

2 *Stories of the stolen children:* Chronological order: attacks on identity (what happened to them) need for understanding (one result), final aim reconciliation (future).

3 *Responses to the* Bringing Them Home *report.* Paraphrase Howard's argument, then contrast to Indigenous perspective.

4 *Later texts:* Indigenous voices, then mainstream media.

I also reorganised my 'theme' notes to reflect the order of topics, treating each theme in each of the four periods.

Step 4: Develop an argument or theme

Now that you have reread your notes and organised your information, you will have some kind of idea about your response. For a home essay, this idea may change as your writing progresses. For exam essays, you are meant to have explored and tested your thoughts already.

The *argument* or theme should constitute the backbone of your essay, the trunk of your tree. This is how an essay can handle complicated, multi-sided topics in a balanced and orderly way. (The more involved your discussion, the better organised it needs to be.) You have seen that I stated my argument in the first paragraph of my essay, and referred back to it regularly in the body, as well as restating it in the conclusion.

Step 5: Plan the essay

Now that you have all the 'ingredients' for an essay, arrange them into a rough plan. While it is preferable to plan before writing your first draft, some people simply can't plan until the first draft has been written. For others, a plan is essential before they can even begin to research the essay. You simply need to experiment and find which ways suit you best. You may even find that you can plan some essays, but not others.

In the exam room it is essential to have a plan of some sort, so you have at least a rough guide to what you want to say before committing yourself to paper.

Plans, like first drafts, are created for yourself, so they can take any form you find helpful. I discuss two very different kinds below:

The keyhole essay plan

This kind of plan does indeed give you the 'key' to the whole essay. The first part opens out the door on the main theme. Then it lists significant topics underneath, and finally broadens out at the end with a statement of conclusion.

(a) Jot down an 'argument statement'— one or two sentences setting out your main idea.

(b) Follow this with the list of topics, noting how they relate to the argument.

(c) Write a concluding statement (if possible).

Keyhole essay plan, *The Stolen Children*

Argument Statement: *The Stolen Children* and other texts give us a privileged perspective on lives subjected to terrible change, and the opportunity to help promote positive change through reconciliation.

1 Historical perspectives suggest that we have always tried to 'conciliate' Aborigines.

2 The stolen children give us a perspective on the effects of attacks on their identity.

3 Some responses from 'official' Australia didn't show real understanding.

4 Since then, official Reconciliation is still faltering despite popular support for it.

Change can be good or bad. It wreaked havoc on the lives of the traditional owners of this continent. Encountering the perspective of the Indigenous people changes our understanding and paves the way for the positive change that symbolic *and* practical Reconciliation should bring.

Other ways of planning: 'mind mapping'

Some writers like to visualise their plan first, literally, so you can draw some kind of diagram if you like. One such method is the *mind map*. You start this in the centre of the page, writing your topic down. The main branches come next, and stem from it directly.

These branches in turn have branches and sub-branches. You can extend these as far as you like, getting as detailed as you wish.

Mind map plan: 'Changing perspectives'

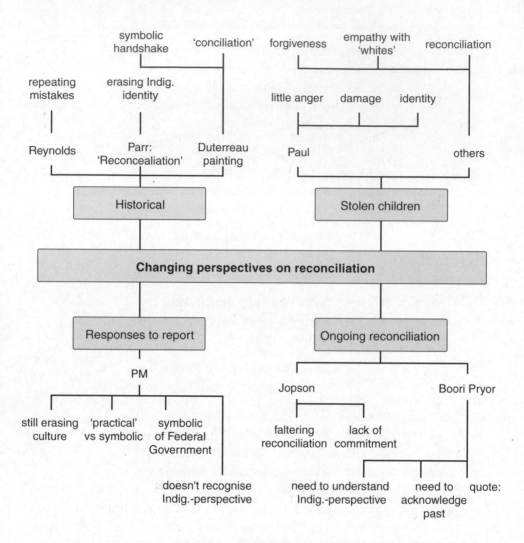

The long walk

Some writers claim that going for a long walk, and planning everything in your head, is essential preparation before putting pen to paper. (Definitely not practical in the exam room however!)

'Audition'

You can even start to plan by talking aloud to a friend, or to a tape recorder!

The structured response

In the 'structured response' type of question, you must respond to a series of questions in order. This can make planning a lot easier. Even when a structured response question isn't used, sometimes the way the question is written suggests a rough outline:

> *Describe the origins of the Delian League. What was its purpose? How successful was it?*

If you're not an Ancient History student and haven't got the faintest idea what the Delian League was, you can still plan an essay. Even if you think that the Delian League is a basketball competition, you can produce a 'correct' plan, useful for guiding research.

Delian League skeleton essay plan

Introduction: Explain what the Delian League was, and how it arose.

Its purpose:

Success: (a) Did it achieve its purpose(s)?
         (b) To what extent, in what ways?
         (c) Evaluation, overall.

Conclusion: Summarise
          Cap off.

Step 6: Draft an introduction

Your introduction has two chief functions;

1 to demonstrate that you have understood the question;

2 to state your argument.

You are ready to start your first draft. Many students complain that the hardest thing is to get started. Once begun, you simply have to follow on the same way, and a good introduction is a reference point you can return to if lost. A well-researched essay can still 'run off the rails' very quickly: you might answer a question on the characters in *1984* with a detailed and insightful account of George Orwell's life and personal philosophy. Wrong!

In exams, it's even more crucial to 'stay on track', because every moment you spend on something irrelevant is time and space lost for material which could earn you marks. In many HSC subjects you will get very little consideration for answers which are off the point. So let's get this introduction right on track.

One way to picture your introduction is as a kind of 'curtain speech':

Think of an old-style drama theatre — you've no doubt seen them in films. There's a grand, plush curtain hiding the stage from us. The houselights dim, and in the dark a spotlight shoots out: the announcer strolls into the light and gives a brief speech telling us what treats are in store tonight, in order of appearance. Thunderous applause, the curtains go up and the show begins.

Your introduction is a 'curtain speech': you *don't* launch straight into the 'main act': first prepare your audience, the readers; get them settled in, let them know what to expect. Only then do you 'raise the curtain' and start discussing your topics in detail. In the 'curtain speech', announce the main ideas but don't give away all the surprises.

The piece of advice allegedly given by a successful preacher in the United States is often repeated: asked the secret of his success, he replied something like this: 'First I tell them what I'm going to say. Then I say it. Then I tell them what I just said'. Introduction, body, conclusion. Your reader will appreciate the courtesy.

(a) 'Echo' the question

Consider your poor teachers and examiners. Reading a pile of essays can become tedious when the writer does not 'signpost'. It is extremely easy to forget something that seems so obvious. It is not enough just to know what you are trying to say or do — it's your job to *communicate*. You can only earn marks for what's in your essay, not what was in your head.

Use the keywords in your introduction. (See the sample essay.) This doesn't mean that you have to rewrite the question, which examiners may find annoying. 'Echoing' has two main advantages:

- the reader can 'tune in' quickly and read with greater ease;

- it shows that you are organised, familiar with the formal, essay structure and that you understand the question.

(b) State your argument

Having demonstrated that you've understood the question, now indicate the argument you are making in response.

(c) Indicate the key points

A mere mention is sufficient at this stage.

Tip. Even when the 'doing' words of the essay question don't ask you to 'define', it can be a very good idea to define any keywords which may be unclear—both for your benefit and that of the reader, who may not be sure what **you** mean by it. For example, a word like 'destiny' will mean something to you, but can you define it adequately? In some subjects, you'll need to go beyond dictionaries to find good definitions of specialised terms.

(d) Anticipate the conclusion (Optional, advanced)

You can go one step beyond stating your initial argument, by indicating your conclusion. (I have done so in the sample essay.)

Step 7: Check your introduction against the checklist

There is a checklist at the end of this chapter. Try to read your introduction objectively, or ask someone else to check it. If it matches the checklist, you've laid the foundations for the entire essay. If not, try to fix this up before proceeding. The words don't have to be perfect, but the direction should be clear.

Step 8: Draft the body of your essay

As we've said, the hardest thing is to 'get going'. But don't forget, when drafting the body of the essay:

- treat each topic in turn;

- sustain your argument;

- refer back to your thesis;

- give specific 'proofs';

- use 'transition' or linking words and phrases;

- paragraph carefully;

- qualify your statements.

Treat each topic in turn

If you have listed your topics or points in the introduction, it's usual to discuss them in the order of listing. This makes it easier to follow the argument.

Sustain your argument

One of the most common weaknesses in student essays is the lack of topic sentences. It's annoying to read a paragraph of discussion with no obvious focus. Don't forget what you're setting out to 'prove', and don't forget to point out how your discussion supports your 'case'.

If you lose track of your argument, try writing a topic sentence for that paragraph. It's a good practice to write a topic sentence at the start of each paragraph, until they become automatic.

Refer back to your argument

Keep returning to your theme. You can avoid restating your argument in full, just by concentrating on keywords.

Give specific 'proofs'

Assertions (statements of fact) are very weak if not supported by 'proof'. Unless what you're saying is definitely well-known or quite obvious, it's better to give details or reasons. (There is no need to prove that there is such a thing as gravity, for instance!) There are many kinds of 'proof': quotes, examples, statistics, use of language, events, the opinions of critics or historians or economists, etc.

Use 'transition' or linking words and phrases

See Chapter 4.

Paragraph carefully

See Chapter 4.

Qualify your statements (advanced skill)

'Qualifying' does not come naturally to us. To 'qualify' means to evaluate or give an opinion rather more carefully than you otherwise might. It is the opposite of being too simplistic, or making sweeping statements about something. Instead of saying that 'Australian writers should write about Australia', reflect that they might also write about overseas experience or events. Avoid statements beginning with: 'Everybody knows that' or 'All … ' unless you are sure of what you're saying.

Consider the weaknesses of your argument before someone else does. Just because your argument has weak points doesn't mean it's invalid, only that (like all things) it has its limits. The ability to consider arguments contrary to your own is actually an impressive skill, well worth developing. The ability to see fine 'shades of grey' is evidence of a perceptive, analytical approach.

Step 9: Draft the conclusion

- Reread essay question.

- Reread introduction.

- Summarise your argument and main points.

- Cap off your argument. .

An impressive conclusion can sometimes make the difference between an average essay and a very good one. Many students seem to have the idea that so long as the introduction and conclusion are okay, the bits in between are just to fill up pages. They might also think that the conclusion is 'basically a summary' and that's all. Wrong on both counts!

Although a conclusion will often start with a summary, the best essays go beyond this. This is the hardest essay-writing skill to teach, but one worth developing when you get more confident. I will at least describe the general idea. (Your conclusion, by the way, does not have to be limited to one paragraph. It can run to several paragraphs. The same goes for introductions. Suit length to the nature of your essay, keeping proportions similar: the bulk of the essay must always be the body.)

You must refer back to the introduction and remind the reader of what we set out to 'discover', 'discuss', 'compare' or 'describe' (for example). So you will again use the keywords.

Finally, don't forget that question: 'So what?' Your conclusion can make further assessments or comparisons, take the argument further or point to its implications. To cap it off in some way makes a valuable final impression and may give you an edge. (The sample essay goes beyond evaluating the history of European/Indigenous relations to look at the future too.)

Some possible 'stings in the tail' are:

- A further consequence of the argument.

- Relating the conclusion to a wider context:
    - implications for the author, character, a question, for our understanding of the work;
    - implications for other works by this author;
    - implications for our understanding of (say) other themes, characters, scenes, etc.;
    - referring to an outside opinion or author.

Step 10: Redraft the essay

As we have discussed, in your first draft the attention is on ideas and facts, on developing your argument, rather than on the words used. All first drafts tend to be 'writer-based': they make perfect sense to ourselves, not necessarily to others yet. In the second draft you must first check the structure, organisation, and the clarity of your argument and concepts, before worrying about the use of language. The work begins of translating that draft into a 'reader-friendly' essay.

Make a fresh start

It is quite difficult to read our own writing 'objectively', as if we were some other reader. But if you've been well organised, and managed to write an early first draft, you can put it away for a couple of days or so, so that you can read it with fresh eyes (the same principle applies to any later drafts too, if you have the luxury of time). Imagine that someone else wrote it, and try to read the draft 'objectively': take note of your immediate reactions when you read because they will often guide you as to what 'works' and what doesn't. Remember that your role is to encourage this writer, so concentrate more on the strong parts than on the weaknesses! The worst thing you can do to this poor person is simply to dismiss their work; your criticism must be constructive, and based on objective questions:

- Is the main argument clear?

- Does there seem to be a point to this essay?

- Are the ideas backed up with evidence?

- Does it actually say what you think it should be saying?

- Do you find it hard to understand what it is saying?

Keep an open mind

An American writing 'guru', William Zinsser has described a 'writing to learn' approach in a book of the same name, based on the idea that in the process of writing you learn by developing your ideas and gaining a truer and deeper understanding. Keep an open mind: above all, it is your job to write a good essay. If it ends up saying what you had wanted it to say, well and good. But be prepared to let it take on a shape of its own if this will create a more accurate, clearer or better argued essay.

If stuck, look again at the data you have collected and organised: what do the facts themselves 'say' to you? What conclusions do they suggest? In subjects other than English, this approach is automatic, but even in English, the argument you choose should come from the 'evidence'. Sometimes it's easier to base your response on the information you do have than to search for facts to support the argument you wanted to develop. And if you can't find much supporting evidence, this suggests that you need to reconsider anyway!

Step 11: Macro-editing

There are two main processes of editing: taking away what does not belong to the essay, and adding whatever else is needed.

Subtraction

Imagine a painting of Sydney Harbour. All the usual beauties are there: Opera House, Harbour Bridge, Circular Quay, and ... Mount Kosciuszko. The mountain touches the whole scene off beautifully—it's well painted and looks great there. Take it away; it doesn't belong. Likewise, take away the bits in your essay that have no relevance: they stand out a mile, they look silly and they'll only lead you astray! It's often tempting to use a favourite quote, to retell the story, or discuss your pet obsession in detail, but leave it out unless it advances your argument in some way.

Addition

It's easier to discover what an essay doesn't need than what it does, but with practice you can develop this skill. A good start is to test whether or not you are supporting each assertion. And if you have 'proved' it sufficiently, have you told us why it matters? So what?

You might, for example, be exploring the fact that Michael Gow's play *Away* is set in the socially turbulent 1960s. This social 'context' is certainly relevant, but you need to explain why or how. Add some supporting evidence from your supplementary reading on the 1960s, about the Vietnam War, about the 'sexual revolution', about R.D. Laing's radical views on psychiatry and mental illness, or from the play itself. Then finally, furnish some consequence or result: 'So what?' For example, if you were writing about Coral's mental illness, you could discuss the appropriateness of Roy's bullying, his headmaster's way of treating her and his unwillingness to allow her to grieve and talk about their dead soldier son, in comparison to 'alternative' viewpoints like Laing's.

It has already been mentioned that some students run out of points to make and use a lot of space just restating their argument. A better strategy is to extend your 'tree trunk' further, or to add new branches.

Some additions that may be appropriate are:

- a quote to support an assertion;
- inserting a topic sentence where a paragraph has none;
- links between paragraphs;
- capping off any paragraph topic, subpoint, or conclusion;
- discussing in greater detail.

Step 12: Micro-editing

When you are reasonably happy with the structure and argument, you should work on improving the language. Many writers find that they keep making improvements to various parts of the essay right up to the final draft. However, in the final draft, your focus will probably be on the fine tuning. Below I discuss a few hints and pointers relating to some of the most common problems.

But be warned: it *is* possible to get very neurotic over an essay and to be unable to 'let it go'. If you find you can't bring yourself to stop fiddling with the final draft, or if you can't bear to hand it up, call your mentor immediately. Tell them it's an emergency! One way of guarding against this danger is to self-evaluate: how many changes did I make in that last redraft? Are they definitely improvements? Why? How important were they? Would they be likely to affect my mark?

Sentence length

I am occasionally asked how long sentences or paragraphs should be. The answer to both questions is: 'as long as they need to be'. The most common problem with long sentences is that the writer is trying to cram in too many ideas. Sometimes they are trying to express several ideas in the one sentence! When in doubt, stick to one main idea per sentence, and treat related ideas in the following sentences.

Many of you will be using a 'grammar checker' with your word processing program. This can be a helpful source of suggestions, but do realise that your own brain is a far more powerful computer than any PC, and most programs can only rely on certain guidelines, which may not be appropriate at all. The final decision must always rest with you, and certainly don't believe everything your computer tells you. There is no grammatical rule about the length of sentences!

On the other hand. Sentences can be too short. This is a problem. Try linking phrases together into longer sentences like this one, instead of writing something like: 'Try linking phrases. Together they can make longer sentences'.

A worse crime, and a very very common one, is the 'run-on sentence'. You should finish a sentence where the thought ends instead of just keeping it going forever even if the thought is quite complete some people just let those words keep flowing on. (And I hope you can see where a full stop should go in the previous sentence!)

Grammar

With grammar, spelling and punctuation, we tend to repeat our mistakes over and over again. Take careful note of all feedback marked on your essays; this is valuable information which should help you to strengthen your writing. Make sure you understand why each mark was made, and if in doubt, ask your teacher for clarification.

Spelling

Good spelling is impressive, and spelling skills will always be a valuable asset to you, if only to save you embarrassment! Spelling is essentially a memory skill, and as we have discussed, the basis of good memory is good organisation and study.

There are a few rules about spelling in English, but because our language is a hybrid of many different languages, there are so many exceptions to these rules that it is almost not worth learning them. One that you certainly should know, however, since so many people have problems here, is: 'i' before 'e' except after 'c'. This will help you spell 'believe' correctly, as well as 'receive' and many other frequently misspelt words.

Make lists of words you have misspelt, and ask someone to test you occasionally. See how many words you can cross off your list by getting them right three times in a row!

One memory trick you can use is to say the word aloud as it is spelt, rather than how it's meant to sound. How would you pronounce the word 'sword' for instance? Another way of remembering is by creating some image or saying: For example 'There are too many o's in the word 'too'.

I've had students tell me smugly that IBM or 'Mac' do all their spelling for them, 'butt eye due knot no foreshore weather spell chequers ah all ways ewes full. Dew yew? Sum wood say their neither hear gnaw they're'. Also, American software can have unreliable ideas about Australian spelling.

Essay editing checklist

Overall

Writer-based or reader-based?
Is there a clear argument?
Is this material relevant?
What further information is needed?
Is this statement backed up with evidence?
Is there an organisational principle ordering the points discussed?
Is the wording clear? (Try it out on someone else.)
How can I express this more clearly?

A: Introduction

Demonstrates an understanding of the question
States the argument
Indicates what topics/points will be discussed
(Optional) Anticipates the conclusion.

B: Body

Paragraphed
Transitions from paragraph to paragraph
Topics treated in order
Argument sustained
Refers back to argument
Detailed, specific 'proofs'
Signposted
Statements qualified.

C: Conclusion

Initial summary
Follows on from
(a) thesis, and

(b) points made.

Capped off: consequences/extra points are observed.

D: Final draft

Word choice

Sentence construction

Grammar

Neat presentation: typed or word processed if possible

Spelling.

sectionthree:

English
essays:
responding
and
composing

Chapter 7

English essays: texts, contexts and the garden of thoughts

Students have often complained to me that with English, unlike every other subject, they don't feel they know what the examiners 'really want' or even how to go about studying it. The approach I outline in this chapter gives you practice with essay writing at the same time as it helps you study for English in an organised fashion.

I remember, when I was young, an older brother proclaiming that his HSC English exams were 'easy'. 'I'd already written my answers in advance' he said. This puzzled me greatly. How *could* he write an essay without knowing what the question was? Impossible! (And, by the way, highly undesirable. Examiners call this trick the 'prepared response', are on guard against it, and treat it ruthlessly. A 'prepared response' either doesn't answer the question, or makes a quick attempt at relating the prepared essay to the question, which generally has very little to do with it.) Obviously my very successful brother hadn't done *that*. So what did he do?

English appears different to most other HSC subjects because there is far less emphasis on 'having the right answer'. This leads some students to the false impression that 'anything goes'. In fact, the best essays in English are the result of careful study and preparation. Even without knowing what question you'll be asked, you can still prepare by developing your own ideas in response to the syllabus requirements. This is your best preparation; and that, I suppose, is what my brother meant.

The best way to prepare for English exams is to write essays: this makes you organise your notes, test and develop your ideas, and read for a purpose. For this reason, I encourage students to base their English study on what I call 'thesis essays'. I'll explain that after first discussing key syllabus requirements.

The HSC English Syllabus

In Mathematics or Science, most of the time, answers are considered to be either objectively right or wrong. In English, one thousand students will write one thousand different answers, all of which can be 'right'. That doesn't necessarily mean that one answer is as good as another; a more helpful distinction is between answers that are well-argued and those that are less well-argued. In theory, you can furnish any reasonable response you like, so long as it's supported by evidence.

> Students are assessed not just on their ideas and knowledge but on how they develop and express them.

It is worthwhile to read the HSC English Stage 6 Syllabus and the syllabus for whichever English course(s) you are studying. These can be found on the Board of Studies' website. You will discover that *meaning* is at the heart of English study, and that this is 'achieved through responding and composing'. That is, you read and study different *texts* (which can include films, multimedia, non-fiction, photographs, paintings, etc.) and formulate a response, which often involves composing an essay. Meaning is not found solely in one text, but between a variety of texts. That is why the syllabus is designed to encourage broad reading of a number of texts and a variety of text types.

For example, the sample essay in Chapter 6 closely analysed the meaning of Geoff Parr's collage in relation to Duterreau's painting. Both of them in turn take on *meaning* in relation to historical, social and political *contexts* such as Indigenous rights and relations with other sectors of Australia. (One way to remember the meaning of 'con-text' is to think of it as the facts and circumstances that are related to, that go 'with' the text. The prefix 'con' usually means 'with'.)

Another central part of the syllabus is the study of language itself, and some useful terms are discussed in the following chapter, which is devoted just to language.

Just as an argument is the backbone of most essays, your response to an English text becomes the basis for an argument and the backbone of your English essay. An argument based on your response to a text can be called a *thesis*, and can be developed into a thesis essay.

Developing your individual response

> Draft a quick essay straight after first reading the text, or viewing the drama, film, or other text.

Shakespeare's tragic character Hamlet had some melancholy things to say about the world, complaining that it seemed to him a 'sterile promontory', a rank 'unweeded garden that grows to seed'. It is easy for your study to become a desert, for your own ideas to wither and die, owing to neglect by starvation, thirst, and general lack of attention. On the other hand, the garden in which your ideas grow can become overgrown with unruly weeds.

The key to English essays is nurturing your best ideas, developing them and weeding out the failures. This process should begin from the moment you first read your English texts. In developing your individual response, you are encouraged to explore the world past and present, through words; other worlds now and then, and the great issues facing us today. English can entertain, amuse, inspire, broaden your mind, fascinate and inform; it can change your life forever. For some of you it is the most enriching study you will ever do — even if you don't realise that now. So while slaving over those books, don't forget to stop and enjoy what you're doing, once in a while at least!

First experience of a text

- Keep a journal, or make a first quick reading, summarise, then read thoroughly.

- Summarise the text after reading it.

- Draft a quick essay based on your ideas.

Your individual response begins with your initial response, so take notes from the moment you read or experience an English *text* (including multimedia, Internet, films, etc.). Keep a journal of your reactions, take notes as you read chapter by chapter, poem by poem, or scene by scene: consider key concerns such as main characters, events, setting in time and place, etc. (For stage and audiovisual texts, similar ideas apply to the production itself.)

Keep asking yourself questions: What is this text about? What is going to happen? Who are the main characters? What are they really like? What are we learning about them? Why does the book start at this point? When you record your answers on an ongoing basis, an initial impression will often be contradicted by a later one: this can be valuable for your notes.

It is a good idea to make a very quick first reading without taking any notes. You should still write about the book as soon as you have finished reading it, and record your initial impressions. Then reread more slowly, taking notes as you go.

If you do prefer the slow reading first, don't let yourself get bogged down at a passage or chapter that is unclear to you. Mark the place with a Post-it note or bookmark, and come back to it after finishing the text. Very often the passage will now make sense to you. If not, ask a teacher, parent or other informed source. Soon after having finished reading, summarise the work in terms of the main characters, setting, story, themes, and so on.

The next step is to write a first essay about that work. This will help you organise your thoughts and start weeding out the vague, half-expressed ideas, while nurturing the stronger ideas. You can follow the method set out below in 'A method for writing thesis essays'. Not only does this give you practice with essay writing but it also provides a very solid foundation for your later study effort on that text, including the work of finding supplementary texts as in the Common Area of Study in English (Standard and Advanced).

Writing and memory

Many students complain that they can never remember anything about a work several weeks after having read it. This doesn't mean they have a 'bad memory', only that they haven't organised themselves to remember. Anyone who can remember their own name, telephone number, and how to drive a car has a perfectly good memory: it's just that they're not using it for specific study purposes yet! As I have said, the key to memory is *organisation*, and good recall is therefore *created* by active study and organisation of thoughts.

One way to remember the 'big picture' is to write about the subject. Unless your first reading and later study are accompanied by note-taking and summaries, you'll forget far too much. Being organised from the start will give you much firmer study foundations to build on.

Computer users know that to prevent their files or documents being lost forever when they turn the computers off, they have to create an appropriate file name, and save this file in an appropriate folder or directory where they'll be able to find it easily. So too must you 'save' your ideas in your own memory: instead of giving them a 'filename' though, you write summaries and brief descriptions, to prevent your knowledge being lost. Keep your loose leaves in separate folders for each English text.

Second reading

It's important to read or otherwise engage with a text at least twice, and poems often need to be read several times, since they can be quite elusive at first. Almost like a problem or puzzle, you may need to 'work them out' for yourself. Many students, faced with a class assignment to write, find that rereading the text without any particular purpose in mind is an excellent way of putting off writing! I have a better suggestion though: if you really have to 'put it off', go out and enjoy yourself. Come back refreshed and ready to really work!

Don't do any work without a clear purpose. If you have written the first draft of an essay *before* rereading, you might surprise yourself by how much you do remember. When in doubt, discuss details from memory, but mark that section of your draft with an asterisk or question mark to remind you to check when you reread. You will find when you do so that your mind absorbs much more, and picks up most of the missing pieces you couldn't remember. Gaps in your memory and understanding, quotes you were looking for but couldn't find, certain events you couldn't remember or weren't clear about, will come into place. You will get a lot more out of it by having a clear purpose, than if you are just rereading, hoping to discover an answer by magic.

The thesis essay study approach

The two chief requirements of HSC English are:

(1) to develop an individual response to a text or unit of work; and
(2) to be able to express it in an organised, well-supported and persuasive manner.

What is a thesis?

We can use another word to summarise the syllabus requirement of responding to a topic or text. Your individual response is developed into a *thesis*.

The word '*thesis*' comes from a Greek word meaning 'to put, set'. It is defined in *The Macquarie Dictionary* as: 'a proposition laid down or stated, especially one to be discussed and proved or to be maintained against objections'. With English you are meant to 'lay down' or state an argument about a text or unit of work. Students often don't realise that they are supposed to find their own thesis, and waste time wondering what the 'right' answer is.

We have already seen that there are two main kinds of question, open and closed. Reread the essay question for the sample essay, in Chapter 6. This open question gives us very little to go on, and we are very much 'thrown back on our own resources'. The key to preparation for such questions is to have developed a thesis for each area of study, module or elective you are undertaking. I have had a running bet with students for years, that I could always relate a good thesis to any exam question, no matter how closed it was. And of course, the more open a question is, the easier it is for you to use your thesis as the basis for an answer.

If essays grow like trees, then your 'thesis' is the seed. Having prepared yourself with notes and study, your 'tree' begins with an idea, which you attempt to 'sprout' in writing, using various facts and quotes to feed it.

> The Thesis Essay Study Method: as soon as you start to study a text or topic, draft a full essay about it, using a 'thesis'—your own response or idea—as an argument.

Advantages of the thesis essay study approach

The thesis essay study approach to English coordinates your notes and summaries by writing a thesis essay on each *topic*. This gives you essential practice with writing, prepares you for class assignments and also provides you with a powerful set of notes.

- It gives you year-long practice in essay writing, so that your writing skills will be well-honed by the time you come to exams. You will also have plenty of time to develop your ideas and find good evidence to support them. You will have the luxury of time to spend on revising, checking facts and quotes, rereading and so on, instead of the futile panic that many students go through.

- Note-taking and reading are done with a purpose, so you will read actively and take notes more efficiently.

- Instead of being piles of 'junk', your notes will be organised into fully articulated ideas.

- You are focused on developing your individual response.

- You are better prepared for class or home assignments throughout the year. By the time an assignment is given out, you have already started thinking about key issues.

- By exam time, although what you hand up is only a first draft, several drafts of essays have gone into organising and testing your ideas on the subject.

- A thesis essay can be written without an essay question having been assigned.

Features of a good thesis

The thesis essay is little different to any other essay, except that instead of being written in answer to a question, it is you who 'asks the question' and decides on what issues or themes to build the argument. In the process of drafting your thesis essay you will be testing out different possibilities. Here are some guides to help you evaluate them.

Centrality

A good thesis is very central to the book. It throws light on, relates to or explains, important aspects of the main characters, events or themes of the work. An argument based solely on sandcastle building in the holiday drama *Away* has almost certainly 'lost the plot'.

Supporting facts

The stronger the thesis, the more evidence we can find to support it, the more this argument and evidence will tell us about the book. For example, I based a thesis essay on the subject of personal growth and development in the play *Six Degrees of Separation*, partly because it reflected the syllabus for the Focus Area 'Changing Self' (2001), and partly because it relates equally well to the three main characters. (The thesis is that personal growth and development are an essential part of life, for adults equally as for children.)

Qualified

We have already talked about 'qualifying' our statements. Likewise, arguments need not be completely 'black and white': the best ones are usually *qualified* in some way. Rather than saying, for example, that '*All* the main characters in *Away* are stunted in their development', you will state your case more carefully: 'Some characters are stunted by mental illness, some by physical illness, some by limited opportunity, and some by rigid attitudes. 'Qualifying' simply means taking account of the limitations of any opinion, and describing as accurately as possible.

Balanced

It is usually preferable to give both sides of the story, thus demonstrating your ability to think critically, to contrast different aspects and to see shades of meaning and complexity. As discussed earlier, the word 'essay' originally meant 'to weigh', and it is common for an argument to 'weigh' both sides of an issue before summing up. Well-balanced theses deserve a favourable reaction.

A method for writing thesis essays

- Reread your notes.
- Brainstorm for ideas.

- Choose the strongest ideas.

- Devise a thesis statement.

- Plan the essay.

- Draft the essay.

As with most essays, the hardest thing is getting started.

1 Reread your notes

Refresh your memory by reading back over your notes and summaries for the text or topic area. (Computer buffs might consider this a bit like loading up important files into RAM!)

2 Brainstorm

Write down every potential thesis idea you can think of: everything that comes up, no matter how silly it sounds. For the time being, concentrate on generating as many ideas as you can—you can weed out the poor ones later. Why not try brainstorming with a group of friends?

Example: You could base a thesis about Louis Nowra's play *Cosi* on one or all of the following themes or issues:

- The difference between madness and sanity

- How art reflects life

- The nature and value of fidelity

- Political activism versus practical social action

- Attitudes to drugs

- How experience changes people

- Different perspectives on the same subject

- Relationships between men and women.

3 Choose the strongest ideas

You now need to choose one key theme for your thesis. You may link several ideas together for this. Now that you have your list, pick through the points and focus on the best. Some other considerations that will guide you are:

- What you know most about

- What you understand best

- What interests you most

- What you consider most important.

If no particular idea stands out, try out the best one, either by proceeding to write more about it, or perhaps discussing it with a friend or teacher. It may be that there is 'something there', but you have yet to find just what it is. Often, indeed almost always, your main 'hunch' has a lot of potential; it may need extra thought and clarification, but will provide you with that all-important starting point.

4 Devise a thesis statement

Write your idea out in full, as an argument statement. (This can be called your 'thesis statement'. You should, preferably, expand on it in the 1-2-3 fashion. Here's an example:

(a) (Guess what?) *Cosi* is a drama all about drama itself, both on stage and off.

(b) (Prove it!) Much of the play is devoted to the development and mounting of an unusual dramatic production, with an unusual cast. But the dramas happening in the everyday lives of its characters are as interesting as the dramas they are portraying on stage.

(c) (So what?) Many of the themes about the nature and purpose of drama can be used to reflect on *Cosi* itself.

5 Organise data

List all the evidence you can find in support of your thesis, under appropriate headings.

6 Plan the essay

Now plan and draft your essay. Instead of being guided by question keywords, however, you should be guided by your own thesis statement, the basis of your argument.

An example of a thesis essay is given below. First, here is a summary of the prescribed text.

SUMMARY OF *SIX DEGREES OF SEPARATION*

Six Degrees of Separation, a drama by John Guare, is the story of an unusual confidence trickster and the effects he has on some people. The confidence trickster, Paul, does not always steal from or otherwise harm his victims; he wants to explore and develop his own potential in an unfamiliar world, the wealthy Upper East Side of New York City, and to gain acceptance there.

Paul is a gay, young Afro-American claiming to be the son of groundbreaking Afro-American actor Sidney Poitier. In preparation for this role, he has learnt to speak like rich people, and to know their values and attitudes. His trick is to have himself invited into their homes by pretending to know the couples' children. These invasions rock the security of the parents and test the relationships between them, and with their children. In the case of private art dealer Flanders Kittredge and his wife Ouisa, his poetic ideas and impressive qualities reverberate within the household long after he has gone, inspiring Ouisa to take a hard look at their life. This may result in a new direction for her, and perhaps for Paul in the future.

In trouble with the law after a later confidence trick, Paul gets back in touch with the Kittredges and is promised support by Ouisa. Tragically for Paul, the Kittredges' efforts to contact him after his arrest are fruitless when the bureaucratic system arbitrarily imposes an absolute 'degree of separation' between them. Ouisa remains determined to remember him, and the final words of the play are her imagined message from Paul, reminding her that their Kandinsky painting is painted 'on two sides'. This suggests that the constrained lives the Kittredges are leading still have potential for personal growth and development if they can find a way to pursue this.

(Note that for the above summary I have kept in mind the syllabus prescriptions for this Focus Area, particularly the central themes of 'Changing Self' and progress or development.)

The following is an edited sample of a thesis essay. Again, it is not perfect, nor a 'model', but should provide some helpful insights into this kind of essay. If the prescribed text and focus area are unfamiliar to you, concentrate on observing the development of the essay's argument, and the various features of the essay, which are discussed in the 'dissected' version that follows.

Sample Thesis Essay: *Six Degrees of Separation*

1 *Six Degrees of Separation* explores the idea that people can and should develop throughout their lives, to avoid the 'emotional and intellectual

paralysis' that its protagonist Paul considers perhaps the 'great modern theme'. It contrasts the lives of two people who suffer arrested development, to the chaotically evolving self of Paul who is yet to reach his potential. In this essay, three strands of Paul's theme are examined: the trap of 'phoney' or stultifying lives, the condition of paralysis or inertia, and the power and importance of imagination. Whether the characters are 'paralysed' like the Kittredges, or too wild like Paul, self-examination and balanced self-development are the necessary steps towards continued growth and self-fulfilment.

2 Paul's ideas are summarised in a key scene where he explains the themes of his supposed university thesis. After dinner, when pressed by his unsuspecting hosts, he examines the popularity of the famous novel *Catcher in the Rye* with some notorious murderers. The novel's hero Holden Caulfield is a teenage boy to whom all adults are 'phoney', who 'wants to do so much and can't do anything'. Paul calls Holden's predicament 'touching' and perhaps relates to the description: 'Hates all phoniness and yet only lies to others'.

3 While his middle-aged audience, Flan and Ouisa Kittredge and their guest Geoffrey listen avidly, they neither imagine that Paul's unlikely alias, of Sidney Poitier's son, might be completely phoney, nor wonder whether their own phoney behaviour, such as flattering their millionaire friend in the hope of a large loan, might not make them one of those people Holden would hate. Ouisa fantasises about herself as an heroic do-gooder devoted to the welfare of black South Africans, and both Kittredges flatter Geoffrey as a martyr to the blacks' political cause, when all we really know is that he owns a lucrative gold mine and has trouble taking his money out of the country.

4 Paul exposes phoney aspects of the Kittredges' own lives, showing how easy it is to penetrate the veneer of upper class culture with flattery and appeals to people's vanity. The play begins the morning after Paul's visit when the Kittredges are reeling in shock after he has threatened their security (by bringing home a hustler), and they briefly dwell on their mortality and thank God. Later they feel humiliation at the way he has exposed their social snobbery (with false appeals to Harvard and Sidney Poitier), gullibility (with the offer to appear in 'Cats') and pseudo-sophisticated lifestyle (by improvising a great pasta in the kitchen and dining better than at the 'Florentine' genius of a local restaurant). Ouisa feared that Paul had spent 'all [his] time laughing at us'.

5 Most importantly, the thinness of their relationships with their children is exposed when the scam is revealed and the kids react with hostility and contempt. Later, when Ouisa suggests that 'Everything is somebody elses' (sic), Paul retorts: 'Not your children. Not your life'. This is a sharp reminder to the Kittredges, whose enjoyment of both is not nearly as good as it should be.

6 It is time for the Kittredges to re-evaluate their lives, because despite their wealth and success, both feel strangely unfulfilled. Ouisa feels 'random' and 'unaccounted for', whereas Flan's dream metaphorically suggests that like painters who 'lose their painting', he too is 'losing' his way in life. In a poignant story Flan recalls asking the second grade art teacher why 'all her students were geniuses'. The first-grade kids made blotchy works, the third graders just 'camouflage', whereas the second grade kids were 'Matisses everyone'. The teacher replies that her secret is knowing 'when to take their drawings away from them'.

7 These three stages could be taken as a metaphor for personal development: first graders are clumsy, chaotic and unformed, whereas third graders have learnt to 'camouflage' themselves in phoney ways and get caught up in overambitious elaboration, losing their way. The goal for both the Kittredges and Paul would be to find their way back to second grade, to achieve a level of expression that is true to themselves without being led astray, without 'losing their paintings'.

8 A bond is formed between Paul and Ouisa because they see each other's real qualities, behind the falseness. Paul tells Ouisa that he knows all about the Kittredges and that they have 'no secrets' from him; yet he finds in them good qualities that lead him to declare he wants their 'everlasting friendship'. Likewise, Ouisa sees much in Paul that is genuine.

> He has this wild quality—yet a real elegance and a real concern and a real consideration.

9 The task for all three main characters is to confront the phoniness in their lives and find an effective way to develop what is real. Paul is still growing and developing, but hasn't yet found his feet. Later he tells Ouisa that his night at the Kittredges was the best night of his life because he had the opportunity to use all parts of himself. This suggests that developing one's own potential is important to greater happiness. For the same reason, what bothers him most about *Catcher in the Rye* is not Holden's bragging and fantasies about violence, but the book's 'aura' of paralysis, which he

defines as 'one of the great tragedies of our time—the death of the imagination'. To Paul, imagination is the 'passport we create to take us to the real world' while also linking us to our 'inner life'. The catastrophic results of his too-free rein of imagination are not a good recommendation, but some of Paul's ideas do indicate a way forward both for himself and for the Kittredges. But first it is helpful to study the nature of the 'paralysis' and inertia that hold the Kittredges back.

10 Paul refers to both intellectual and emotional paralysis and the Kittredges show signs of both in their lack of imagination, and sterile family life. However, Paul's words echo in their 'inner lives', the realm that has starved ever since 'imagination has become a synonym for style', and so there is hope for them. In Ouisa's first dream, 'Sidney Poitier' complains that society devotes too much attention to the 'bookends' of birth and death, too little to 'the eighty years in between'—that is, life itself.

11 A quote from the playwright Samuel Beckett, one of the great dramatists of paralysis according to Paul, offers us a clue. In his play *Endgame*, focused on the twilight days of a wheelchair-bound old man, Hamm, the younger figure Clov asks: 'Do you believe in the life to come?' and Hamm responds: 'Mine was always that'. This bleak response deflects the question away from 'eternal life' to the way we live on earth. For Flan and Ouisa, the life to come consists of a predictable series of paintings that Flan will buy and sell, bringing them greater and greater wealth, and predictable career paths for their Harvard-educated children. But at present their life is always 'the life to come' since they are not living it fully now.

12 Flan too faces his intellectual and emotional paralysis in a dream, a stirring in his own 'inner life':

> —And I thought—dreamed—remembered—how easy it is for a painter to *lose* a painting. He can paint and paint—work on a canvas for months and one day he loses it—just loses the structure—loses the sense of it—you lose the painting.

This dream is a metaphor for a person losing their true self, or their way in life: Flan too works and works, slaves and schemes away at his art dealing and not only 'loses the painting' literally, every time he secures a treasure and resells it, but over time has lost his appreciation of art and the many possibilities life holds. The dream offers him hope as he listens to his inner life and feels close to the paintings that he presently sells like 'pieces of meat'.

13 By the end of the play, however, little has changed in their lives. Ouisa reaches out emotionally to Paul before he is arrested, but her efforts end in paralysis. Although he has faced the reality of his life as a 'gambler', Flan continues as before, and both parents put their needy daughter Tess 'on hold' because of other pressing matters. Ouisa's frustration is clear. When she asks Flan how much of *his* life he can account for, he simply refers to his success and riches. With similar desperation to Tess, who threatens to ruin her life and 'throw away everything you want me to be because it's the only way to hurt you', Ouisa says to Flan: 'These are the times I would take a knife and dig out your heart'. The intellectual and emotional paralysis is yet to be overcome.

14 Playwright John Guare consistently uses painting and art as metaphors for life. At the start of the play the two-sided Kandinsky revolves slowly, displaying both its 'geometric and sombre' and its 'wild and vivid' sides. The former side, on which it finally rests, corresponds to the formal and sober life of money, lawyers, bankers and 'schmoozing' clients, that the Kittredges lead. The wild and vivid side of the Kandinsky corresponds to Paul's extravagant ways. Neither side, in isolation, brings a balanced life of self-fulfilment. Imagination alone is not enough; nor is material success, unless it is balanced with intellectual and emotional engagement.

15 During the confronting scene towards the end where Ouisa is reviewing their lives, Flan praises renowned painter Cezanne because he deals with the problem Ouisa faces of 'keeping the experience'. Each of Cezanne's brushstrokes has a purpose, whereas Ouisa feels 'all random', her life a 'collage of unaccounted-for brushstrokes'. Flan's viewpoint tells only half the story, however, and it is actually Paul who makes the most insightful comment, in passing, when he explains to Elizabeth that 'Cezanne looked for the rules behind the spontaneity of Impressionism'. In other words, Cezanne combined the inputs of 'both sides of the painting': he subjected his wilder, imaginative, more spontaneous side to the need for structure (discipline) and an understanding of what he was doing. This is what people need to do in life too, so as to develop in a balanced way.

16 The Kittredges suffer from a lack of spontaneity and vividness in their lives, as Paul reminds her in another dream scene:

> The imagination. That's our out. Our imagination teaches us our limits and then how to grow beyond those limits … If we don't listen to that voice, it dies. It shrivels. It vanishes.

Paul, with his imagination and wild ways is in no such danger, but he leaves a trail of damage to others which finally sees him, too, caught in a paralysis: prison life. Both the Kittredges and Paul need to find a way to combine both 'sides of the painting' in their lives.

17 Paul 'adopts' two fathers as role models. He could rise to acclaim from humble and disadvantaged beginnings like Sidney Poitier, or he could become a successful art dealer like Flan. Ouisa scolds him for being both 'so smart and so stupid', for not realising what he could be, and Paul asks her for the help that might give him the guidance of 'the rules'. He secures a number of promises that could help set him up for life if he survives prison. In return, Paul can offer the Kittredges his imagination, youth, life experience and those other 'real qualities' Ouisa noted. Paul, who Ouisa admiringly calls a 'Columbus', a 'Magellan', would agree with Sigmund Freud that 'there's no such thing as luck. Just what you make.'

18 Likewise the Kittredges can be guided to develop their emotional and intellectual lives. Ouisa feels the frustration of those tantalising few 'degrees of separation' that both divide her from and could connect her to, all people in the world. To her, each new person is a 'door' onto new worlds. Flan too may get back to 'second grade' if he is prepared to face himself and listen to his inner voice. At present, however, like the narrator of 'Sky-high' in the Stimulus booklet *Change*, there are 'too many things tying [him] to the ground'.

19 Paul alerts the Kittredges to the phoney and meaningless lives they are leading, and offers them a way out through 'imagination' if they are prepared to face the 'hard part'.

> To face ourselves. That's the hard thing. The imagination. That's God's gift to make the act of self-examination bearable.

At the same time, Paul himself indulges 'God's gift' too much and probably hasn't yet 'faced himself'.

20 By the end of the play the Kittredges are still paralysed, but Ouisa is determined not to lose Paul's insights. As she tells Flan:

> But it was an experience. I will not turn him into an anecdote .... We become these human jukeboxes spilling out these anecdotes. But it was an experience. How do we *keep* the experience?

In the final words of the play, Paul reminds her: 'The Kandinsky. It's painted on both sides'. As the Kandinsky suggests, there are at least two sides to the work of anyone's life, and we shouldn't turn our back on either. A fulfilling life involves intellectual and emotional growth. All three characters must face themselves, abandon phoney ways and balance imagination with discipline, to have a life that is not 'the life to come' nor random brushstrokes, but a life in the 'real world' that unpacks their own potential.

(Note how easily this thesis essay could be adapted to the essay question in Chapter 6. The response could argue something like: 'My understanding of change has been shaped in reading *Six Degrees of Separation* and other texts, by discovering that change as personal development is an essential part of life, not just for young adults but for older people too.')

'Dissected' version of the sample thesis essay

The same essay is now reprinted with notes. As with the previous essay in Chapter 6:

- Headings are inserted, for guidance.

- Paragraphs are numbered.

- The key parts of topic sentences are <u>underlined</u>.

- The argument statement is <u>double underlined</u>.

- Comments are in *italics*.

- Aspect keywords are in `reverse type`.

Because there is no essay question, there are no question keywords. `Aspect keywords` relate to key parts of the argument.

Sample Thesis Essay: *Six degrees of separation*

Introduction

1 *Six Degrees of Separation* explores the idea that <u>people can and should `develop` throughout their lives</u>, to avoid the 'emotional and intellectual `paralysis`' that its protagonist Paul considers perhaps the 'great modern theme'. It contrasts the lives of two people who suffer arrested

development, to the chaotically evolving self of Paul who is yet to reach his potential. In this essay, three strands of Paul's theme are examined: the trap of 'phoney' or stultifying lives, the condition of paralysis or inertia, and the power and importance of imagination . Whether the characters are 'paralysed' like the Kittredges, or too wild like Paul, <u>self-examination and balanced self-development are the necessary steps towards continued growth and self-fulfilment</u>.

This paragraph immediately introduces the aspect words that relate to the thesis, just as essays written in response to a question echo the keywords and state an argument. You should get straight to the point and set up the essay here. This first paragraph lists three strands of the argument, which will be discussed in turn as well as announcing the argument. Since my thesis was developed in response to the 2001 Common Area of Study Focus Area 'Changing Self', growth and development of the self are two important aspects. Other aspects were suggested by the play itself.

SECTION 1: PHONEY/STULTIFYING LIVES

2 <u>Paul's ideas are summarised in a key scene where he explains the content of his</u> supposed <u>university thesis</u>, After dinner, when pressed by his unsuspecting hosts, he examines the popularity of the famous novel *Catcher in the Rye* with some notorious murderers. The novel's hero Holden Caulfield is a teenage boy to whom all adults are 'phoney' , who 'wants to do so much and can't do anything'. Paul calls Holden's predicament 'touching' and perhaps relates to the description: 'Hates all phoniness and yet only lies to others'.

Because Paul's speech is so central to my argument, I've devoted this first paragraph on the first strand of the argument to sketching the context of Paul's ideas.

3 While his middle-aged audience, <u>Flan and Ouisa Kittredge</u> and their guest Geoffrey listen avidly, they <u>neither imagine that Paul's unlikely alias,</u> of Sidney Poitier's son, might be <u>completely</u> 'phoney' , nor wonder whether their <u>own phoney behaviour,</u> such as flattering their millionaire friend in the hope of a large loan, might not make them one of those people Holden would hate. Ouisa fantasises about herself as an heroic do-gooder devoted to the welfare of black South Africans, and both Kittredges flatter Geoffrey as a martyr to the blacks' political cause, when all we really know is that he owns a lucrative gold mine and has trouble taking his money out of the country.

My next step is to apply the central term under discussion, 'phoniness', to all three main characters, who will be closely compared throughout.

4 Paul's exposes **'phoney'** aspects of the Kittredges' own lives, showing how easy it is to penetrate the veneer of upper class culture with flattery and appeals to people's vanity. The play begins the morning after Paul's visit when the Kittredges are reeling in shock after Paul has threatened their security (by bringing home a hustler), and they briefly dwell on their mortality and thank God. Later they feel humiliation at the way he has exposed their social snobbery (with false appeals to Harvard and Sidney Poitier), gullibility (with the offer to appear in 'Cats') and pseudo-sophisticated lifestyle (by improvising a great pasta in the kitchen and dining better than at the 'Florentine' genius of a local restaurant). Ouisa feared that Paul had spent 'all [his] time laughing at us'.

The discussion of 'phoniness' now gets more detailed.

5 Most importantly, the thinness of their relationships with their children is exposed when the scam is revealed and the kids react with hostility and contempt. Later, when Ouisa suggests that 'Everything is somebody elses'(sic), Paul retorts: 'Not your children. Not your life'. This is a sharp reminder to the Kittredges, whose enjoyment of both is not nearly as good as it should be.

Detailed discussion of 'phoniness' ends with the single most important example. Quotes are always used in relation to the argument, never just for the sake of it! The Latin word 'sic' (thus) is used to signify that any error or anomaly was in the original quotation.

6 It is time for the Kittredges to re-evaluate their lives, because despite their wealth and success, both feel strangely unfulfilled. Ouisa feels 'random' and 'unaccounted for', whereas Flan's dream metaphorically suggests that like painters who 'lose their painting', he too is 'losing' his way in life. In a poignant story Flan recalls asking the second grade art teacher why 'all her students were geniuses'. The first-grade kids made blotchy works, the third graders just 'camouflage', whereas the second grade kids were 'Matisses everyone'. The teacher replies that her secret is knowing 'when to take their drawings away from them'.

The argument now develops from having established 'phoniness', to explain 'so what?' That is, why is a 'phoney' life a problem?

7 These three stages could be taken as a metaphor for personal development : first graders are clumsy, chaotic and unformed, whereas third graders have learnt to 'camouflage' themselves in phoney ways and get caught up in overambitious elaboration, losing their way. The goal for both the Kittredges and Paul would be to find their way back to second grade, to achieve a level of expression that is true to themselves without being led astray, without 'losing their paintings'.

Now that the problem of emptiness/unfulfilment has been explained, the next logical step is to contrast with a preferable state of existence: 'second grade'.

8 A bond is formed between Paul and Ouisa because they see each other's real qualities, behind the falseness . Paul tells Ouisa that he knows all about the Kittredges and that they have 'no secrets' from him; yet he finds in them good qualities that lead him to declare he wants their 'everlasting friendship'. Likewise, Ouisa sees much in Paul that is genuine.

> He has this wild quality—yet a real elegance and a real concern and a real consideration.

The final logical point is to demonstrate that something can be done about phoniness, so the discussion turns to 'real' qualities in these characters.

9 The task for all three main characters is to confront the phoniness in their lives and find an effective way to develop what is real. Paul is still growing and developing, but hasn't yet found his feet. Later he tells Ouisa that his night at the Kittredges was the best night of his life because he had the opportunity to use all parts of himself. This suggests that developing one's own potential is important to greater happiness. For the same reason, what bothers him most about *Catcher in the Rye* is not Holden's bragging and fantasies about violence, but the book's 'aura' of paralysis , which he defines as 'one of the great tragedies of our time— the death of the imagination '. To Paul, imagination is the 'passport we create to take us to the real world' while also linking us to our 'inner life'. The catastrophic results of his too-free rein of imagination are not a good recommendation but some of Paul's ideas do indicate a way forward both for himself and for the Kittredges. But first it is helpful to study the nature of the 'paralysis' and inertia that hold the Kittredges back.

The final paragraph of this first section gives a mini-summary: phoniness for the three characters results in unfulfilment and the need for self-

development. It then relates the preceding discussion to the other two key strands of the argument, imagination and paralysis, to tie the discussion to this argument, finally signposting the next section.

Section 2: Paralysis/inertia

10 <u>Paul refers to both intellectual and emotional</u> paralysis <u>and the Kittredges show signs of both</u> in their lack of imagination, and sterile family life. However, Paul's words echo in their 'inner lives', the realm that has starved ever since ' imagination has become a synonym for style', and so there is hope for them. In Ouisa's first dream, 'Sidney Poitier' complains that society devotes too much attention to the 'bookends' of birth and death, too little to 'the eighty years in between'—that is, life itself.

This paragraph broadly introduces 'paralysis' in its two forms, in relation to Flan and Ouisa.

11 A quote from the playwright Samuel Beckett, one of the great dramatists of paralysis according to Paul, offers us a clue. In his play *Endgame*, focused on the twilight days of a wheelchair-bound old man, Hamm, the younger figure Clov asks: 'Do you believe in the life to come?' and Hamm responds: 'Mine was always that'. This bleak response deflects the question away from 'eternal life' to the way we live on earth. For Flan and Ouisa, the life to come consists of a predictable series of paintings that Flan will buy and sell, bringing them greater and greater wealth, and predictable career paths for their Harvard-educated children. <u>But at present their life is always 'the life to come' since they are not living it fully now.</u>

This continues the broad discussion in reference to a text of my own choosing, since the English syllabus specifies wider reading in the Common Area of Study. There are unlimited possibilities for wider texts. Art students could research painting techniques, individual paintings or some of the famous painters the dramatist refers to. One can research absurdist plays, Catcher in the Rye, *and so on. The film* American Beauty *also has much to offer. One of the benefits of a thesis essay is that it can 'grow' all year as you read more and have additional details and texts to refer to. For example, one could make additional notes about language and form, as the syllabus specifies for this Focus Area. To keep this sample essay shorter, I make only passing reference to some of these other texts throughout the essay.*

12 Flan too faces his intellectual and emotional paralysis in a dream, a stirring in his own 'inner life':

—And I thought—dreamed—remembered—how easy it is for a painter to *lose* a painting. He can paint and paint—work on a canvas for months and one day he loses it—just loses the structure—loses the sense of it— you lose the painting.

<u>This dream is a metaphor for a person losing their true self, or their way in life</u>: Flan too works and works, slaves and schemes away at his art dealing and not only 'loses the painting' literally, every time he secures a treasure and resells it, but over time has lost his appreciation of art and the many possibilities life holds. The dream offers him hope as he listens to his inner life and feels close to the paintings that he presently sells like 'pieces of meat'.

More detail about paralysis is discussed.

13 <u>By the end of the play, however, little has changed in their lives</u>. Ouisa reaches out emotionally to Paul before he is arrested, but her efforts end in paralysis . Although he has faced the reality of his life as a 'gambler', Flan continues as before, and both parents put their needy daughter Tess 'on hold' because of other pressing matters. Ouisa's frustration is clear. When she asks Flan how much of *his* life he can account for, he simply refers to his success and riches. With similar desperation to Tess, who threatens to ruin her life and 'throw away everything you want me to be because it's the only way to hurt you', Ouisa says to Flan: 'These are the times I would take a knife and dig out your heart'. The intellectual and emotional paralysis are yet to be overcome.

The final paragraph of the section sums up. I haven't linked to the next section, 'imagination', because this connection has already been established.

Section 3: Importance of imagination

14 Playwright John Guare consistently uses painting and art as metaphors for life. At the start of the play the two-sided Kandinsky revolves slowly, displaying both its 'geometric and sombre' and its 'wild and vivid' sides. The former side, on which it finally rests, corresponds to the formal and sober life of money, lawyers, bankers and 'schmoozing' clients, that the Kittredges lead. The wild and vivid side of the Kandinsky corresponds to Paul's extravagant ways. Neither side, in isolation, brings a balanced life of self-fulfilment. Imagination <u>alone is not enough; nor is material success, unless it is balanced with intellectual and emotional engagement</u>.

The final sentence here prepares the ground for the argument of the following paragraph.

15 During the confronting scene towards the end where Ouisa is reviewing their lives, Flan praises renowned painter Cezanne, because he deals with the problem Ouisa faces, of 'keeping the experience'. Each of Cezanne's brushstrokes has a purpose, whereas Ouisa feels 'all random', her life a 'collage of unaccounted-for brushstrokes'. Flan's viewpoint tells only half the story, however, and it is actually Paul who makes the most insightful comment, in passing, when he explains to Elizabeth that 'Cezanne looked for the rules behind the spontaneity of Impressionism'. In other words, <u>Cezanne combined the inputs of 'both sides of the painting'</u>: he subjected his wilder, imaginative , more spontaneous side to the need for structure (discipline) and an understanding of what he was doing. This is what people need to do in life too, so as to develop in a balanced way.

The final two sentences above establish the argument on 'imagination' which is supported in the following two paragraphs and linked to other aspects of the essay's argument.

16 The Kittredges suffer from a lack of spontaneity and vividness in their lives, as Paul reminds her in another dream scene:

> The imagination. That's our out. Our imagination teaches us our limits and then how to grow beyond those limits … If we don't listen to that voice, it dies. It shrivels. It vanishes.

Paul, with his imagination and wild ways is in no such danger, but he leaves a trail of damage to others which finally sees him, too, caught in a paralysis : prison life. <u>Both the Kittredges and Paul need to find a way to combine both 'sides of the painting' in their lives</u>.

The argument is now linked from 'imagination' back to paralysis, and in the following paragraph, to self-development.

17 Paul 'adopts' two fathers as role models. He could rise to acclaim from humble and disadvantaged beginnings like Sidney Poitier, or he could become a successful art dealer like Flan. Ouisa scolds him for being both 'so smart and so stupid', for not realising what he could be, and Paul asks her for the help that might give him the guidance of 'the rules'. He secures a number of promises that could help set him up for life if he survives prison. In return, Paul can offer the Kittredges his imagination , youth, life experience and those other 'real' qualities Ouisa noted. <u>Paul</u>, who

Ouisa admiringly calls a 'Columbus', a 'Magellan', would agree with Sigmund Freud that 'there's no such thing as luck. Just what you make.'

18 Likewise the Kittredges can be guided to develop their emotional and intellectual lives. Ouisa feels the frustration of those tantalising few 'degrees of separation' that both divide her from and could connect her to, all people in the world. To her, each new person is a 'door' onto new worlds. Flan too may get back to 'second grade' if he is prepared to face himself and listen to his inner voice. At present, however, like the narrator of 'Sky-high' in the Stimulus booklet *Change*, there are 'too many things tying [him] to the ground'.

The complete version of this essay would discuss some relevant texts from the 2001 Stimulus Booklet 'Change' as it is a compulsory text. The short narrative 'Sky-High' and Miroslav Holub's poem 'The Door', have obvious relevance here. The sample essay in Chapter 6 gives examples of how to incorporate such material.

CONCLUSION

19 Paul alerts the Kittredges to the `phoney` and meaningless lives they are leading, and offers them a way out through `'imagination'` if they are prepared to face the 'hard part'.

> To face ourselves. That's the hard thing. The imagination. That's God's gift to make the act of self-examination bearable.

At the same time, Paul himself indulges 'God's gift' too much and probably hasn't yet 'faced himself'.

The conclusion begins with a summary of what has been demonstrated, relating it all back to the key aspect of 'imagination'.

20 By the end of the play the Kittredges are still `paralysed`, but Ouisa is determined not to lose Paul's insights. As she tells Flan:

> But it was an experience. I will not turn him into an anecdote .... We become these human jukeboxes spilling out these anecdotes. But it was an experience. How do we *keep* the experience?

In the final words of the play, Paul reminds her: 'The Kandinsky. It's painted on both sides'. As the Kandinsky suggests, there are at least two sides to the work of anyone's life, and we shouldn't turn our back on either. A fulfilling life involves intellectual and emotional `growth`. All three characters must face themselves, abandon ██phoney██ ways and balance ██imagination██ with discipline, to have a life that is not 'the life to come' nor random brushstrokes, but a life in the 'real world' that unpacks their own ██potential██.

This conclusion restates the thesis argument, tying it to the points that have been discussed in the body of the essay, and 'caps off' with two quotes that support the argument forcefully. The quotes from Ouisa and Paul represent two very different perspectives from 'both sides of the painting'.

EXERCISES

1 Look at old HSC papers, and find questions on texts you are studying (your school library, or local library, should have these). If you can't find any, make up your own based on a question for a similar text: drama, poetry, or novel. Sketch out a rough plan for an essay to answer it. Before starting, note whether the question is 'open' or 'closed'.

2 Write a thesis essay for the most recent English text you've read.

3 Do one for each English text you have studied so far.

Chapter 8

(What is this thing called) language

Language, language, language

In HSC English, your essays are marked not merely on your knowledge and ideas, but also on your use of the right essay structure and your ability to use language to express yourself. As you draft and redraft essays, the work you put in to polish word choice and expression will pay off doubly, as your thoughts become clearer and more precise, and your better use of language creates a favourable impression.

There's another strong reason why you need to become more aware of language: language itself is a central part of the syllabus. The syllabus requires that you respond to and compose different types of language usage in different *genres* (kinds of writing), to write in different styles, at different *registers* (levels) of formality (from formal essay English to other registers), and across a variety of forms. Becoming more aware of language also gives you extra 'ammunition' and support for your argument. For example, in the sample essay of Chapter 6 I analysed both visual language (a painting and a collage) and the verbal language of stories and speeches. Each form, such as drama, film and multimedia, has its own language, and so do different genres.

Of course we all know what language is … we use it all the time. You're using it right now as you read. It seems as automatic as breathing the air. And yet, how much do we actually know about language? (How much does the average person really know about air, or breathing for that matter?) When it comes to questions asking you to discuss the use of language in a reading passage, or as part of an essay question, many students have virtually no idea what is expected.

When asked to comment on language, students often just look for similes and metaphors, and perhaps imagery. These forms are called 'figurative' language, and yes, they are *examples* of language usage, but language is far more than that.

What is 'language'?

Language is *what the words are saying* and *how they express it*. That is a definition worth committing to memory, because it explains that language can be virtually any aspect of a text. When you examine language, you should start by examining the meanings it represents, secondly looking at the ways it works. Language is not just 'words', and literary devices, but their meaning, their effect. Without considering the meaning conveyed by words, language is—well—meaningless! 'Language' is also the structure of a text, the genre in which it is written, the conventions and codes it uses, and any means of communicating a message, which may include very subtle ways.

> **LANGUAGE IS:**
>
> 1 Words
> 2 What they mean
> 3 The effect they have
> 4 How they are used to get the meaning across.

Language of viewing and representation

The English syllabus considers multimedia, films, paintings and photographs as 'texts'. The language they use goes beyond words, and can draw on whole other systems, codes and conventions, to convey meaning. An introductory list would include the following:

Non-verbal communication: (for various media)
body language   tone of voice
facial expressions   gesture
dress

Painting/other artworks:

perspective	colours
brushstroke	foregrounding
juxtaposition	collage
balance of elements	

Film language:

composition of the frame

the different kinds of camera shots: close-up, medium close-up, etc., tracking shots, dolly shots

editing

transitions between scenes: fades, wipes, dissolves, etc.

montage (editing technique of juxtaposing a series of images to make meaning)

framing: what's in the frame, and what is not

Multimedia:

sound	hyperlinks
menu	film and other graphic material

Word choice

Professional writers, especially creative writers, use words very carefully. It was Samuel Taylor Coleridge who advised looking at a piece of writing and asking: how would the meaning be altered if one word (or several) were changed? Ask yourself how an idea could have been expressed differently? What effect would this have had? Why did the writer employ this precise choice of words?

Reading and language (read read read, write write write)

In a radio interview broadcast not long before his death, Australia's Nobel prizewinning author Patrick White was asked what advice he would give to budding writers:

'Read read read. Write write write' was his reply. The more you read, not only is your store of knowledge enriched, but your familiarity with language is enhanced. Reading and writing are two sides of the one coin. Quite apart from whatever else you learn, you are learning about language every time you read.

Of course, the more knowledge you have, the better support you'll be able to give to your arguments in all subjects. In English you are expected to find supplementary materials in a variety of genres, which may include:

- Clippings from newspapers and magazines

- Internet sites

- Promotional or informational brochures from various organisations

- TV or radio broadcasts

- Non-fiction books on a study area

- Critical writings: collections or single articles on an author or work

- Film, radio or stage adaptations.

Critics and commentaries

HSC students are not expected to become 'critics' themselves, but you may find it very helpful to look at some critical writings, commentaries or study guides on a work or author. (For example, Pascal publishes an excellent series of 'Studies in Literature' on HSC English texts.) Any of these resources can provide helpful background information and fresh insights. In general, don't forget to criticise the critics too. This doesn't mean to 'knock' them, but to be aware of possible defects in their arguments.

Some language terms

In terms of 'proving' a thesis or other argument, some of the best evidence you can provide in an English essay is discussion of language. You don't just quote a passage but you must also examine details, explaining what you think it *means* and *how* words are used to express this.

Your notes on each text should include samples of language and discussion of its effects. I have provided a list of helpful language terms below. Familiarising yourself with them will expand your repertoire of language discussion skills—and help you become more aware of your own usage!

Antithesis Use of contrasting terms in conjunction.

Contrast   Directly comparing different matters to highlight differences.

Devices Any means used by the writer to achieve a particular effect, such as:
— suspense
— drama
— plot
— jokes
— incongruity (things being 'out of place').

Genre The type of writing used, or the particular activity for which it is used. Priests use language differently to police, a recipe uses language differently to a fan letter, a birthday greeting is different to an obituary. Literary genres include westerns, science fiction, romance, thrillers, and so on. It's important to realise that the purpose for which language is used will directly affect the use of language. A romance novel is unlikely to use heavy philosophical concepts, nor will it use the pseudo-scientific jargon of 'Sci Fi'. Each genre has its own conventions, which help to distinguish it from others.

Onomatopoeia The sound of the word imitates the sound to which it refers, for example 'splash', 'beep'.

Oxymoron A contradiction in terms: for example, 'honest criminal'.

Paradox An apparent contradiction. Ted Hughes' 'Jaguar' is encaged and yet feels free.

Parallelism The sustained drawing out of two similar stories or characters with common elements; for example, the theme of fidelity in Mozart's *Cosi Fan Tutte* is paralleled by the same theme in the lives of Lewis, Henry and others, in *Cosi*.

Point of view The standpoint from which the piece is written. Who is telling the story: is the narrator speaking in the first or third person? From whose point of view is *Looking for Alibrandi* written? *Life is Beautiful? Things Fall Apart?* Does the narrator know all, or is his or her knowledge limited? Is the standpoint historical or contemporary?

Pun A play on words. Puns are often based on words that sound similar, or that have similar meanings. 'Many are cold but few are frozen', puns on a well-known saying. 'Life depends on the liver' has two quite separate meanings, both of which may be intended at the same time.

Purpose   What is the writer attempting to convey, and to whom? For example: **didactic** works are intended to teach; propaganda aims to persuade for political purposes. Other purposes are: to be frivolous, entertaining, amusing, informative. And so on!

Register   The 'level' of language used. An academic or a diplomat uses a high, formal register. An essay uses formal language, not slang. Some journalists use very simple language, others employ a higher register.

Rhythm   Does the language have a particular rhythm or does it use a particular form, such as blank verse, a limerick, a sonnet, etc?

Style   How the language is 'dressed'. Styles can be simple or complex, wordy or concise, 'mannered' or direct, flowing or staccato ('jerky').

Tone   The writer's *attitude* to the subject matter (a very important consideration, which you will often be asked to comment upon). Examples: humorous, ironic (extremely common, but tricky), sarcastic, didactic, playful, mocking, emotional, angry, loving, eulogistic, morbid, conversational, absurd, quirky, zany.

Vocabulary   The reservoir of words from which we choose. Vocabulary is an immensely helpful asset in language. You can never know too many words. Some people certainly have richer vocabularies than others, but the good news is that these riches come absolutely free! There are times when one word will sum up so much: Look up the word *altruistic* if you don't know it already. It's defined in my *Macquarie Dictionary* as 'The principle or practice of seeking the welfare of others'. In other words, an altruist is an unselfish person motivated to look after people. It takes many words to explain the idea though, doesn't it! The word 'unselfish' doesn't quite express the same meaning, or in as much detail. To learn a new word is often to learn a new concept as well!

The renowned French novelist Marcel Proust valued words so highly that he devised an extreme way of learning new ones. He'd write them on strips of paper and hang them with pegs on a clothes line in his room. Why not try bluetacking new words all over the house, on your bedroom mirror … see how long it takes to infuriate your parents or flatmates! (For enthusiasts only, but you probably wouldn't be the first student to do it!)

Word choice The bigger your vocabulary, the richer are your opportunities for word use. When analysing a writer's use of language, consider why one word was used in preference to another. What other words could have been used, and how would this have affected the meaning?

Figures of speech

Figurative language is language that is not literal, (that is, not intended to be 'taken for real'), but is used for effect. Such language is heavily used by poets, but is also common elsewhere.

Metaphor An important and extremely common figure of speech, it is where 'one thing is described in terms of another'. Paul writes in *The Stolen Children* that 'my shadow was my best friend'. This powerful metaphor expresses his lonely and empty life. This figure of speech is so important that I've taken it out of alphabetical order to put it at the top of the list!

Hyperbole A gross exaggeration: 'Millions of people came to the end-of-school-year party last night'.

Imagery We normally refer to imagery as 'painting a picture with words' but actually it can appeal to any of the five senses. Poet Bruce Dawe uses much imagery in the garden of 'Homo Suburbiensis': 'the hoarse rasping tendrils of pumpkin flourish clumsy whips and their foliage sprawls …'

Irony Saying something other than what you intend people to understand. We could mean the opposite ('lovely day' during a storm), or we could be using *understatement*. For example 'I didn't try too hard' might mean 'I didn't try at all'.

Metonymy A detail is used to represent the whole: For example 'I saw three sails on the horizon' means 'ships', not sails.

Simile   Like metaphors, similes are a comparison, but they use 'like' or 'as'. Metaphors are a comparison where we say that one item *is* another. For example:

Simile: 'This film is like a roller coaster ride.'

Metaphor: 'This film is a roller coaster ride.'

What different *effects* do these two versions have on you, the reader?

SOME FURTHER LANGUAGE VOCABULARY

Effect	Anti-climax	Objective
Evoke	Sequence	Subjective
Atmosphere	Feelings	Theme
Compare	Connotation	Issue
Structure	Denotation	

sectionfour:

Study hints and subject guide

Chapter 9

Exams, and essays in other subjects

So: if a good essay takes several drafts, how can you be expected to write an 'extended response' in 40 minutes and one draft only, in the exam room? Good question. First, don't panic: examiners are aware of this issue, and take it into account. Secondly, everyone's in the same position. Thirdly, you can prepare yourself for exams by 'rehearsing' with old exam papers, timing yourself and working under exam-like conditions, by writing draft exam essays and by organising your study well.

There are several important differences between exam essays and other essays:

- There is a strict time limit (and, although you are not marked according to the length of your essay, a detailed, complete essay does impress).

- You don't have time to polish a rough draft.

- You can't research. (That is why your study must be as well organised as possible beforehand.)

- Planning is essential, because there is no time to change your argument midway through the essay.

Exam strategies

- Read the entire paper quickly. Start to think about which questions you'll do, and how to answer them.

- Try outlining a quick essay plan for each question before you start to answer any. Sometimes, forgotten information or 'inspiration' will come to your aid when you return to that question. It's as if the unconscious mind works on automatic pilot!

- If you get stuck with one essay, go on to the others before coming back to it.

- Make sure you read ALL instructions and follow them exactly (it's easy to overlook something important).

- Know in advance how much time is allowed for each question, and stick to it. It may be tempting to write extra material on one question, but the gains you could make will be minimal compared to the marks you might lose in the next question.

- Some questions are split into a number of different parts, each with a separate weighting of marks. Look at what each question is worth and tailor the length of your response and the amount of time you spend on it, accordingly. If a question is worth twelve marks, and part (a) is worth three marks, you should spend about a quarter of the total time allocated to that question on part (a).

- Make doubly sure that you answer ALL of the question. If the question makes two or more demands, answer all of them.

- Try to leave a minute or so to check back over each essay, fixing up any glaring omissions or errors.

As one example of meeting exam requirements, here are some hints for treating the English Standard papers.

(*Note*: the following hints are based on the 2001 Specimen Papers. The format of these exam papers may change so you should check.)

Exam hints: English (Standard and Advanced) Paper 1: Area of Study

Time management: Paper 1 involves answering three questions, 40 minutes allowed per question, with a total of ten minutes additional reading time.

Note that the paper should state briefly, at the head of each section, what you will be assessed on.

SECTION I

This section involves reading unseen texts related to the Area of Study and consists of a number of shorter responses.

Don't assume that it is adequate to give the 'right answer' in just a few words. Assume that the examiner will be unconvinced until you demonstrate your comprehension fully using the three-step method (see Chapter 4). The more marks the question is worth, the more your answer needs to be complete and satisfying.

Other hints

- Read or examine all the texts and all the questions before answering. Try to determine the overall *tone* — the author's attitude to the subject matter — and the theme or opinion being developed.

- Take careful note of the mark allocation per question; these vary considerably.

- Answer questions with reference to the *context* of the text(s). Often the context of a phrase or detail will indicate a different meaning from dictionary or everyday meanings.

- Make sure your answer is from the *text(s)* rather than from your general knowledge!

- Pass over and return to the 'too hard' questions: they may 'click into place' once you've progressed further and relaxed a bit more.

- You may find it helpful to mark relevant passages on the exam paper, to make it easier to find answers.

SECTION II

In this section you are required to compose (write) or adapt (change) a text for a specific purpose. Knowledge of a wide variety of forms of writing (genres) will help greatly, enriching your general knowledge, your vocabulary and understanding of the different features of different genres. Expect the unexpected!

Always write with a clear purpose. This will help you stand out from those writers who just pour out ideas haphazardly. The instructions will indicate what is required.

You can practise for this section by writing pieces that vary the use of register, purpose, form, format, audience, role and vocabulary. You might be asked to write a letter, an interview, a play script or some other piece, or to produce a piece for a specific magazine and suggest accompanying graphics. Whatever the task, suit the language to the genre of writing.

You can practise your command of *register* by writing dialogue for two different characters requiring different kinds of speech: for example, compare a politician's public speech with her or his normal speech at home, or compare 'street-kid' speech with a businessperson's on the same subject.

Examples of different genres:

Thriller novels	Comedy sketches	Political speeches
Autobiographies	Press releases	Obituaries
TV news broadcasts	Encyclopaedia entries	Hypertext writing
Recipes	Government reports	Advertisements
Diaries	Cartoons	Love letters
Feature articles	Drama scripts	Hypertext novels
Song lyrics	Eulogies	Editorials
Film reviews	Fan letters	Raps

Section III

This section involves an extended response to a question based on the Area of Study, and generally in the form of an essay, unless otherwise specified. You may or may not be specifically asked to refer to the prescribed text and Stimulus Booklet, but it is generally advisable to do so.

Gathering a range of supplementary material is also important as it allows you greater scope in your response. Materials can be gleaned from a very wide range of sources, including newspapers, magazines, radio or television broadcasts, brochures from government or private organisations, library collections, audiovisual or multimedia sources, interviews, etc.

English (Standard) Paper 2: Modules

This paper is worth 60 marks, compared to Paper 1 (40 marks).

Time management: Three questions, each of equal value. Forty minutes should be allocated to each question, and there is an additional five minutes reading time for the paper. Each question requires an 'extended response'.

This paper should state briefly, at the head of each section, what you will be assessed on.

Essay writing in other subjects

While this book focuses on the essay or extended response in English, all the skills you practise will aid your writing in short responses, in other genres (such as reports) and in other HSC subjects also. Contrary to what many people imagine, the English essay makes as many demands as any other kind, as the specified outcomes in the syllabus make explicit. The best English essays are analytical and critical, detailed and specific; they interpret and explain relevant facts and ideas. In fact, English is especially demanding since it emphasises not only your knowledge of the topic, but also your ability to formulate an individual response and to use language well.

However, don't assume that expectations are identical in each HSC subject, since the essay can take different forms and operate under different rules. Pay careful attention to your teacher's stipulations, and don't hesitate to ask questions if you are still unsure. (Some subjects allow you to include headings and graphs, for example.) Once you have mastered the techniques in this book, you will have little trouble in customising your writing to somewhat different expectations.

Assessment in each subject is focused on the specified outcomes. In many, the emphasis is on your knowledge and understanding of the subject, your ability to explain and discuss issues and topics in relation to appropriate theories, concepts, practices and systems of thought (e.g. the law), rather than on your opinion or individual response.

Extended-response questions may be in the form of a structured response, which requires you to answer a series of questions in order. The individual parts of these questions may each attract separate marks, the final question often being worth the greatest number of marks.

A number of students have successfully adapted the 'thesis essay' idea to other subjects: Economics, Ancient and Modern History, Legal Studies, etc. If you prepare for such exams in this way, bear in mind that the examiner is more interested in your knowledge and understanding than in your personal response, and don't try to simply regurgitate a prepared essay!

Non-argument essay modes

We have seen that the basis of essays in HSC English is the *argument*, around which the essay is structured. However, *argument* is only one of four writing modes. Essays and other formal writings commonly use the other three modes too: *description, exposition* (explanation), and *narration*. In other subjects, depending on the question, you might use one or more of these modes. It is not uncommon for an essay to use all four modes, in different sections.

Two of these modes can be prescribed in essay questions, where you are required to 'describe' or 'explain' in some detail. Generally you should still consider using the standard essay structure. Other common prescribed 'doing words' are 'evaluate', 'analyse', 'assess' and 'discuss'. Often it is necessary to *describe, explain* or *narrate* in order to communicate your knowledge and understanding, before proceeding to evaluate, analyse, assess or discuss.

Familiarising yourself with the meaning of these 'doing words' as defined in a glossary by the Board of Studies, and becoming aware of these other modes, will help you meet the expectations of your writing. A selection from that glossary is reproduced at the end of this chapter.

Description

The Board of Studies defines the instruction word 'describe' as 'provide characteristics and features'. Bear in mind that this describing should be relevant to the question.

> Describe important aspects of chemical usage that need to be considered to provide safeguards to the farm environment.
>
> (Adapted from 2001 HSC Specimen Paper, Agriculture, Board of Studies NSW)

One could write an essay in response to this question, establishing a theme or argument, then in the body *describing* 'important aspects'. Here is a sample essay outline:

Introduction

> Chemicals have many positive uses and can be indispensable to many farmers.
> If not used correctly, they can have implications for:
> 1 occupational health and safety of farm workers;
> 2 farm environment generally;
> 3 contaminating produce and hurting sales and profitability.
> So various practices and precautions need to be followed.

Body

1 *Describe* the benefits of chemical usage.
2 *Describe* the positive aspects of chemical usage.
3 Dangers:
   (a) Occupational health and safety: *Describe* how chemical usage affects it.
   (b) Farm environment: *Describe* chemical usage's possible effects.
4 *Describe* the results of carelessness or abuse of chemical usage.

Conclusion

Briefly restate the theme based on discussion.

Cap off: Chemicals are very useful but can endanger the farm environment.

The key is their proper usage and disposal.

In such an essay, you would use the mode of *description* for much of the essay, but still use the usual essay format, basing it on a theme.

Although the following question does not ask you to *describe*, description is implied:

> Evaluate traditional and contemporary approaches to the management and protection of one ecosystem you have studied and one ecosystem evident in the Stimulus Booklet.
>
> (2001 HSC Specimen Paper, Geography, Board of Studies NSW).

Before *evaluating*, you need to *describe* different approaches to the management and protection of two separate ecosystems.

Exposition: (explaining)

'Explain' is defined by the Board of Studies as 'relate cause and effect; make the relationship between things evident; provide why and/or how.'

> Explain how an individual economy (other than Australia) is endeavouring to promote its level of economic development, in an environment where globalisation is affecting living standards.
>
> (2001 HSC Specimen Paper, Economics, Board of Studies NSW).

In the above essay, much of the body would be devoted to *explaining* an economy's efforts to promote its economic development, and perhaps *describing* the environment of globalisation and its effects on living standards.

The following is a possible essay outline (based on a fictional economy).

Introduction

The economy of Troglia is attempting to promote its economic development in the following ways:

- economic reform program suggested by World Bank;
- taking advantage of freed-up trade opportunities;
- attracting investment capital for target industries;
- promoting tourism.

Body

- *Explain* the benefits of economic reform for economic development.
- *Explain* how freer trade can aid economic development.
- *Explain* the role of target industries in promoting economic development.
- *Explain* the value of tourism for economic development.

Conclusion

Globalisation offers challenges and benefits to Troglia. Troglia is responding so as to maximise its opportunities for economic development.

Narration

Like 'argument', narration is a mode that is unlikely to be specified in the 'doing words' of an essay question. However, at times it is helpful to 'tell a story': to give historical background to an event or phenomenon, to explain the sequence of events, or to narrate how you conducted primary research. If the main argument of the sample essay in Chapter 6 were that it is essential to tell the story of the past so as to embrace the future, the series of texts could have been treated in relation to a continuous *narrative* from the first day of the European invasion of Australia, through various changes up to the present.

Suggestions for other subjects

The following are some general suggestions to help you come to grips with the particular requirements of essays in subjects other than English:

- You are marked not merely on your knowledge and on your ability to present that knowledge in a well-structured, sustained way, but specifically on the designated outcomes for each unit of study you take. Become familiar with these outcomes and with the marking 'rubrics' that guide your markers. (This information can be found at the Board of Studies' website.) Criteria might include: wide range of sources, using up-to-date sources, ability to make use of the stimulus text, and understanding of key concepts.

- It is especially important to *shape* and *structure* your response according to the question and target outcomes, not to get bogged down in mere data for the sake of it.

- Pay close attention to the 'doing words' in the question.

- Consult specialised study guides for that subject.

- Read past examination papers, and the specimen papers available on the Board of Studies' website.

- Study actively, always thinking about themes and issues. Ask questions as you study. Interpret information: what significance do these statistics have? What are the implications? How do they affect my ideas about this topic? Does this source agree with other sources, or contradict them?

- Practise on previous exam papers in that subject, under exam conditions.

- Go over all your returned assessments: What are your strengths and weaknesses, and how can you improve both? Ask your teacher for additional feedback if necessary.

- For assignments, keep within specified word limits unless your teacher states otherwise. (Ten per cent allowance either way is generally acceptable.)

Structured-response exam questions

An example of a structured-response question is the following:

Question 9 — Heritage and Identity (30 marks)

(a) Using the source above and your own knowledge, answer the following:

(i) Explain how indigenous art has been exploited for commercial gain.

(ii) What does the NIAAA spokesman mean in his last sentence as it relates to Aboriginal art?

(b) To what extent have contemporary expressions of Aboriginal heritage and identity contributed to the strengthening of Aboriginal culture? Use your Local Aboriginal Community Case Study in your answer.

(2001 HSC Specimen Paper, Aboriginal Studies, Board of Studies NSW)

In this example, the question is worth 30 marks and the first two parts in (a) are worth 5 marks each. That leaves 20 marks for part (b), in which you would write an 'extended response'. Your essay could develop an argument based on the evidence of your Case Study.

Subject-specific tips

Geography

An unusual form of essay you might use in assignments is the pictorial essay, based on various visual stimuli, rather than on words. Make sure that all visual items are titled and referenced.

Ancient and Modern History

Wide reading is especially important in history, as is your ability to analyse data critically. Whereas English encourages you to compose in various written genres, and different registers, history consistently expects a formal quality of language.

Society and Culture

In this subject, as in all subjects, it is important to use the relevant terms and language, to 'think' in that language. You may need to write about Primary research (your original research), Secondary research, or both. Depending on the question, it may be appropriate to use a more personal tone in passages where you reflect on your own experience, for example in relation to the Personal Reflection methodology.

Select glossary of instruction words

Account: Account for: state reasons for, report on. Give an account of: narrate a series of events or transactions.

Analyse: Identify components and the relationship between them; draw out and relate implications.

Apply: Use, utilise, employ in a particular situation.

Assess: Make a judgement of value, quality, outcomes, results or size.

Calculate: Ascertain/determine from given facts, figures or information.

Compare: Show how things are similar or different.

Contrast: Show how things are different or opposite.

Critically (analyse/evaluate): Add a degree or level of accuracy, depth, knowledge and understanding, questioning, reflection and quality to (analysis/evaluation).

Define: State meaning and identify essential qualities.

Demonstrate: Show by example.

Describe: Provide characteristics and features.

Discuss: Identify issues and provide points for and/or against.

Distinguish: Recognise or note/indicate as being distinct or different from; to note differences between.

Evaluate: Make a judgement based on criteria; determine the value of.

Examine: Inquire into.

Explain: Relate cause and effect; make the relationships between things evident; provide why and/or how.

Interpret: Draw meaning from.

Outline: Sketch in general terms; indicate the main features of.

Summarise: Express, concisely, the relevant details.

Synthesise: Put together various elements to make a whole.

This is a selection from a comprehensive list of instruction words, available from the Board of Studies website at http://www.boardofstudies.nsw.edu.au.

Chapter 10

Final hints

Improve your language use

When checking over all returned work, if you don't understand why a correction was made, ask the teacher how the essay could have been improved.

- Get straight to the point! Long, vague strings of words only give the impression that you have nothing to say.

- Don't try to cram a whole paragaph into one sentence: language comes easier when you deal with thoughts one at a time.

- You can experiment by imitating writers you admire. Try to follow their style and structures, not what they are saying! Don't worry about being 'too' influenced: most writers start off emulating their 'heroes', but the more books you read, the less debt you will owe to any one particular writer.

- Learn five spellings a day, starting with your most frequent errors.

Some practical tips

- Keep essay drafts until the assignment is finished. This can give you confidence to experiment with later drafts, knowing that you're not 'losing' previous work.

Computers

If you have a home computer, remove all games from the hard disk (if they pose too great a temptation) and use word processing software for your assignments. You may find it helpful to do most of your note-taking and writing on computer.

You may find it a good idea to save your early draft assignments under a new name, and in a subdirectory or folder named 'earlierdrafts', for example. You could save a Bruce Dawe essay as 'DAWEDRAFT1.DOC', etc. That way you can always refer back to your work rather than having to delete earlier versions and possibly deleting paragraphs that you might later decide you need. Looking at earlier drafts is often reassuring as you can measure your progress, and it is a good feeling to realise that you now have a better understanding of the topic than at the time of writing the first draft.

Make sure you back up all your files (make copies of them) and keep 'hard copies' (printouts) as well, for safety.

> *Tip*: Some students get stuck on their original essay draft, always trying to base their next draft on the previous one, slavishly copying out whole paragraphs again under the impression that it is saving them extra work. Sometimes you are better off 'letting it go' and starting completely anew. You have nothing to lose by trying it, but by all means save the older drafts if it will help to reassure you.

Study groups

Study can be more fun, and often far more productive, if done in study groups. You can swap notes about a work or author, read each other's essays constructively, discuss language and ideas. When giving feedback to others you should:

- Emphasise the positive aspects of the essay first.

- Critically scrutinise the facts and structure, but *never* the writer.

- Never take criticism of your writing personally.

Other assistance

Some TAFEs, evening colleges, and even universities offer essay-writing workshops from time to time where you can work on your skills with a group of people sharing common interests. TAFE students can seek help at Individual Learning Centres, where tuition is offered to anyone wanting help. Perhaps your school has some support to offer, or could be persuaded to run workshops for a group of interested classmates after school.

Motivation

Write a checklist outlining all the work you feel you should do in order to study each subject properly. Make a conscious decision about how much you would like to achieve. For Standard English, you might plan to:

- Read all texts at least twice.

- Write a thesis essay for each text, relating to the prescribed perspectives of the Study Area or Module.

- Take notes on major characters and events.

- Gather some key quotes and relate them to your thesis.

- See live productions of dramas you are studying, or their film adaptations.

- Find and read supplementary materials relating to the Area of Study and any modules where this will help.

- Read criticism, and/or read biographies of authors.

- Consult study guides for specific texts.

- Allocate the last few weeks before the exams solely to revision.

- Set goals for yourself to finish specific tasks by a certain (realistic) time and *stick to it*, no matter what!

And don't listen to that terrible voice of temptation whispering in your ear … 'You can always go back and do the HSC again next year …' Tell yourself right now, 'I can't!' Who wants to lose another year of their life? Next year you could be out making money in a job, or studying the course that will get you where you want to be!

Enjoyment

Although the HSC may resemble a kind of medieval torture to you, it also represents a great opportunity for you to explore the world through study, at a time when your mind is developing rapidly. Students often write much better essays on a book or poet they enjoy. Why do you think that is so?

Even if you didn't like a text at first reading, try to find something of value in it. If it's not the kind of book you would 'normally' read, open your mind, and try to see what value it might have for you and for others. Talk to someone who does like that book, and find out why!

And remember when studying an English text, that fiction, drama and poetry are written for the *enjoyment* or enlightenment of others! If you're not 'getting it' then it's worth asking yourself why not.

For teachers, marking a pile of essays can be rather hard work, and it is always appreciated when a zestful, original piece comes onto the desk! Like most endeavours in life, you only get out of writing what you put into it. By now you should realise that essay writing is a skill that asks you for many inputs: your study, your writing 'microskills', your understanding of the essay form, and your ability to express yourself clearly in language. Beyond that, your individual response will sometimes cast up a gem that your teacher will find most worthwhile and enjoyable to read. It is much more likely to happen when you are genuinely exploring the subject yourself. Good luck with your studies!

Select bibliography

Macquarie Dictionary is a fine Australian dictionary. Other good dictionaries include Chambers *Twentieth Century Dictionary* and the *Oxford Concise Dictionary*.

Thesauruses

Thesauruses are helpful in looking for precise words, or an alternative word, by meaning. A good recent edition is:

B. Kirkpatrick (ed.)(1987), *The Authorised Roget's Thesaurus*, Penguin, London.

Grammar

A.J. Taylor (1990) *Chambers English Grammar*, Chambers, Edinburgh.

Punctuation

A short but valuable work on this important subject:

Whitaker-Wilson, C. (1975), *Punctuation*, Sun Books, South Melbourne.

On Writing

L. Flower (1993) (4th edition) *Problem Solving strategies for Writing*, Harcourt Brace Jovanovich, Fort Worth.

H. Klauser (1987) *Writing on Both Sides of the Brain*, Harper and Row, San Francisco.

W. Zinsser (1988) *Writing to Learn*, Harper and Row, New York.

Board of Studies website

There is a wealth of up-to-date information on this website, including specimen exam papers, previous exam papers, syllabus documents and so on.

http://www.boardofstudies.nsw.edu.au